Is It Ethical? 101 Scenarios in Everyday Social Work Practice
A Discussion Workbook

by Thomas Horn, MSW, RSW

White Hat **Communications**

Harrisburg, Pennsylvania

Published by: White Hat **Communications**

Post Office Box 5390
Harrisburg, PA 17110-0390 U.S.A.
717-238-3787 (voice)
717-238-2090 (fax)
http://www.socialworker.com and http://shop.whitehatcommunications.com

Copyright © 2011 by Thomas Horn

Front cover photograph © 2011 Marek Uliasz. Image from BigStockPhoto.com.

Library of Congress Cataloging-in-Publication Data

Horn, Thomas, 1968-
    Is it ethical? : 101 scenarios in everyday social work practice : a discussion workbook / by Thomas Horn.
        p. cm.
    Includes index.
    ISBN 978-1-929109-29-6
    1. Social workers—Professional ethics. 2. Social service—Moral and ethical aspects. I. Title.
    HV10.5.H65 2011
    174'.93613—dc22
                                        2011009456

Is It Ethical? 101 Scenarios in Everyday Social Work Practice
A Discussion Workbook

Table of Contents

Introduction

Professional ethics is an extremely important topic for human services professionals, and it is essential to be mindful of the range of dilemmas we can find ourselves in while practicing in this field. I believe that the vast majority of social work interns and practicing social workers are honest, have integrity, and really do consider the needs of a client first.

Very few of us go to work looking for ways to exploit, manipulate, or mislead the people with whom we work, be they clients, colleagues, managers, the government, or the general public. Instead, I think when people cross into unethical behavior, it is often a series of poor decisions that are misguided, and we lose our moral and professional direction. The line between ethical and unethical can become blurred. We can get too wrapped up in the moment to recognize the impact of our decisions.

Sometimes the best move is to step back, take a breath, look at the big picture, and consult colleagues. In other words, taking a break and waiting to make a decision can be much better than making a poor one. Unfortunately, our pride, stubbornness, and overconfidence can get in the way of clarity of thought and wise decisions. Honesty with ourselves and the use of the consultative process can prevent many of the sad and shameful ethical breaches that we often hear about in our line of work. One of the tests for assessing ethical behavior is to ask whether another reasonable social worker, under the same set of circumstances, would make the same decision as you. With continued reading, practice, and discussion, I hope we can all become that reasonable social worker.

I wrote this workbook for use within academic and professional settings to engage people in discussion and to debate as to where the ethical line is set, recognizing that it can move over time, setting, and circumstance. It should be noted that there can be and are differences between what is illegal behavior, what is labeled as unethical behavior according to a written standard (usually found within a code of ethics and/or standards of professional practice), and what is generally considered unethical in a broader sense. This workbook provides a range of scenarios that can be found in everyday professional social work settings that may or may not be illegal, unethical, or against the code that you follow. In some cases, the behavior(s) within a scenario may be against the policies and procedures of an organization or may be "politically incorrect," but may not necessarily be "unethical."

Blank space is provided after each scenario so you can write out your own thoughts, opinions, and emotional reactions, or you might want to write them out elsewhere. It would be most beneficial to share your thoughts and opinions with others, either in a classroom setting, team meeting, or with friends or colleagues after school or work. Discussing these ethical scenarios with friends not working in or studying social services would be very interesting, as well, because they may have a different take on what is ethical and/or acceptable professional behavior (e.g., some might think sex between a client and a psychotherapist is fine, not recognizing the multiple problems with it).

It would be a good idea to have a copy of the code of ethics that you are required to follow handy, so you can refer to it when needed. In all cases, the hypothetical workers named in these scenarios are regulated health professionals, all fully licensed or registered social workers, bound by a code of ethics that is consistent with international standards. The scenarios are presented in no particular order and could happen anywhere.

Please also note that all names and scenarios used in this guidebook are fictional or based loosely on the author's experiences/exposure and are not meant to refer to any specific event, location, or person, living or dead. Any similarities are coincidental.

Thomas Horn, MSW, RSW

Scenarios

1

Mary is a clinical social worker who has lived in the same small town her whole life and, as a result, she and her family are connected to numerous other families in the community. She is the only social worker in the town, and it is an hour's drive to the nearest city, which has a clinic providing similar services. Her hairdresser, who has been cutting and styling her hair for years, asked Mary if she could see her through her private practice to work on issues related to her deteriorating marriage. Mary agrees.

- Is it ethical for Mary to provide services to her hairdresser?
- If *no*, please explain why not. What does Mary need to do to ensure clear, ethical boundaries in this relationship?
- If *yes*, explain your position. If she is breaching the code of ethics that you are required to follow, describe all possible breaches with reference to the applicable section numbers within the standards of practice guidelines.
- Try to understand why others may disagree with you. What might be their argument?

My response:

2

Fatima is self-employed with her own private practice. She has recently gone on a marketing blitz, with new ads in the phone book and on the Internet. She has developed her own Web site that describes her services and promotes her work. Fatima has many satisfied clients and has asked some of them to provide testimonials for her great service, so she can include them on her Web site.

* Is Fatima advertising in an ethical manner?
* If it *is* ethical, please explain your position. What must she do to ensure informed consent and privacy?
* If it *is not* ethical, explain your position. If she is breaching the code of ethics that you are required to follow, describe all possible breaches with reference to the applicable section numbers within the standards of practice guidelines.
* Could there be any pressure felt by these previous/current clients to agree to provide testimonials, even if they are not comfortable doing so? Please explain.

My response:

3

Bob is a lonely social worker who has a secret crush on a female client he has seen for the past three months regarding her depressed mood. On several occasions during their weekly sessions, he has asked her intimate questions about her sex life, including questions about masturbation. She has never objected.

- Is Bob acting ethically?
- If his actions *are* ethical, give your reasoning. What would he need to do to ensure that he does not cross "the line"?
- If his actions *are not* ethical, explain your position. If he is breaching the code of ethics that you are required to follow, describe all possible breaches with reference to the applicable section numbers within the standards of practice guidelines.
- Why might the client not object if she is feeling uncomfortable?
- If Bob kept his sexualized thoughts to himself and was otherwise appropriate in his behavior, would this be ethical? Why or why not?
- If Bob did keep his sexualized thoughts to himself, but being a dutiful clinician shared them with his supervisor, what might the consequences be, positive or negative?
- If you had inappropriate sexual thoughts about a client, would you share them with your supervisor?

My response:

4

Cynthia is an outpatient therapist at a hospital and has a client she sees for an apparent obsessive-compulsive disorder. The client is a successful businessman with several companies, and he offers her an unbelievable chance to invest in a company he just started that has the potential to make millions. Cynthia refuses to talk about it during the session, but she arranges to meet him for coffee after work. She decides to invest in this new company.

- Is Cynthia engaging in ethical behavior?
- If she *is*, explain your reasoning. Do you have suggestions for her so that she remains ethical?
- If she *is not*, explain your position. If she is breaching the code of ethics that you are required to follow, describe all possible breaches with reference to the applicable section numbers within the standards of practice guidelines.
- How might this arrangement affect their therapeutic relationship? What might happen if she ends up losing her life savings?

My response:

5

Mohammed is an out-of-work social worker who was just turned down by five employers in one week. When he finds out about a dream position at a nearby agency, he decides to embellish his résumé. He claims to possess certification in an area he has read about extensively. He has years of experience, but has no official training or certification in this area.

- Is Mohammed acting in an ethical manner?
- If his actions are *ethical*, please explain why.
- If they are *unethical*, describe your position. If he is breaching the code of ethics that you are required to follow, describe all possible breaches with reference to the applicable section numbers within the standards of practice guidelines.
- What if Mohammed purposely *removed* significant education or experience from his résumé because he considered himself "over-qualified" for a position?

My response:

6

Marlene works on an acute psychiatry ward and has been told by both the psychiatrist and the unit manager that a particular patient must be discharged within the hour to free up a bed. She believes that this patient is not ready for discharge, given that he continues to be actively suicidal. The patient is homeless, has no social supports, and no follow-up has been arranged. He has been banned by all local shelters because of his past threatening behavior. He has been on the unit for the past 72 hours, but the psychiatrist will not re-certify him and does not want him as a voluntary patient. The patient wants to continue the work he started with the social worker, Marlene, however. She decides not to challenge the decision to discharge, because she is afraid of being fired or at the very least getting blacklisted by the hospital. Security escorts the patient out to the street within the hour with just the clothing on his back.

- Was Marlene's behavior (or lack of action) ethical? NO
- If *yes*, explain how she maintained ethical standards.
- If *no*, share your reasons. If she breached the code of ethics that you are required to follow, describe all possible breaches with reference to the applicable section numbers within the standards of practice guidelines.
- Would it have been ethical for Marlene to give the patient her business card and suggest he call her, so she can help him "off the record"? Why or why not?
- Try to understand why others may disagree with you. What might be their argument?

> **My response:**
>
>
>
>
>
>
>
>
>
>
>

7

Balwinder refers a chronically addicted client to a private drug treatment center that has no waitlist. The next week, he is surprised to receive a $100 check in the mail from the center, with a note thanking him for the business. With a smile on his face, Balwinder deposits the unexpected, but welcome, check into his personal bank account.

- Was it ethical for Balwinder to accept the check?
- If it *was*, explain why that is your opinion.
- If it *was not*, what is your reasoning? If he did breach the code of ethics that you are required to follow, describe all possible breaches with reference to the applicable section numbers within the standards of practice guidelines.
- Would it make a difference if the check was for $5 rather than $100?

My response:

8

Jason is an assistant professor in the school of social work at a fairly large university. He sometimes uses the department photocopier for personal use and does not tell anyone that it was not work-related.

* Is it ethical for Jason to act in this way?
* If it *is*, please share your reasoning.
* If it *is not* ethical, explain why not. If Jason is breaching the code of ethics that you are required to follow, describe all possible breaches with reference to the applicable section numbers within the standards of practice guidelines.
* Would it make a difference if he made just one copy? What about 1,000?

My response:

9

Paola is a school social worker. As she is driving home from work during a rain storm, she sees a female student she counseled last year, huddled alone at a bus stop, totally soaked and shivering. She decides to pull over and offer the girl a ride.

- Did Paola make an ethically sound decision?
- If *yes*, please share your reasoning. What does she need to do to ensure ethics are maintained?
- If *no*, explain your position. If Paola did breach the code of ethics that you are required to follow, describe all possible breaches with reference to the applicable section numbers within the standards of practice guidelines.
- Would it have made a difference if the student was male? What if the social worker was male?

My response:

10

Carlos is an outreach social worker who stopped to chat with a homeless man he has known for several years. The man appeared to be quite drunk, so Carlos offered to take him to the local detoxification center. This angered the man, who started to yell and wave his arms in an aggressive manner. Carlos persisted, trying to explain that it is warm in the center and he can get some food there. The man responded by hitting Carlos square in the jaw. Given Carlos' years of boxing, he instinctively punched the man back in the nose.

- Did Carlos act in an unethical manner? Yes
- If he *did not*, explain why his actions were justified. Was it self-defense?
- If he *did*, please share your position. If he breached the code of ethics that you are required to follow, describe all possible breaches with reference to the applicable section numbers within the standards of practice guidelines.
- Could Carlos have done something different to change this chain of events?
- Try to understand why others may disagree with you. What might be their argument?

My response:

May not be reproduced without permission of the publisher. Please use additional sheets if necessary.

11

Steve is a hospital social worker with training in the management of aggressive behavior, including the use of physical restraint, the same as all other front-line staff at the hospital. When a code alarm is sounded, signaling that there is an aggressive patient and staff or patients are in danger, he responds along with staff members from several other units. By the time Steve arrives on the scene, the patient is already being restrained on the floor by several staff members. The manner of restraint is not endorsed by the hospital, because the position could physically harm or even kill the patient. Those restraining him then decide to carry the patient to an isolation room, which is done in a dangerous manner not even close to the hospital policy. While the patient is being carried, a female staff member has difficulty holding one of his legs, which is thrashing violently. Steve grabs and holds the foot to protect the staff member from getting kicked while they walk to the seclusion room.

- Is Steve's behavior ethical?
- If it is *ethical*, please share your reasoning.
- If his behavior is *unethical*, explain your position. If he breached the code of ethics that you are required to follow, describe all possible breaches with reference to the applicable section numbers within the standards of practice guidelines.
- As a peer, did Steve have any authority or responsibility to tell the staff to position themselves and the patient differently to follow policy (and good/best practice)?
- What possible consequences might exist for Steve if the patient dies during the restraint or transport and Steve is identified as one of the staff who assisted?
- What possible consequences, official or not, could Steve face for not backing up the staff member who was seriously kicked because he did not grab the foot?

My response:

12

Emily likes taking her pre-teen children to the neighborhood mall after work. While walking with them, she sees a client of hers across the food court. Emily waves vigorously at the woman and yells out, "Hi, Susan!" She then explains to her children that Susan is a client of hers from work.

- Is it ethical for Emily to act in this manner?
- If *yes*, explain why.
- If *no*, share your position. If she did breach the code of ethics that you are required to follow, describe all possible breaches with reference to the applicable section numbers within the standards of practice guidelines.
- If you decided that it was an unethical act, would your mind change if Susan, the client, was happy to see Emily and her children and did not mind at all?
- How might you feel if you were Emily's client and she did this to you?
- What, if any, impact might this incident have on the therapeutic relationship between Emily and Susan?

My response:

13

Frank is a social worker at an outpatient mental health clinic with operating hours from 8:30 a.m. to 5:00 p.m., Monday through Friday. One of his regular clients calls at 4:30 p.m. on Wednesday asking for an urgent appointment to see him at 5:30 that day, at a time when the clinic is closed and all the office staff and other clinicians have gone home. Rather than referring him to the crisis clinic, which is open 24 hours per day, or squeezing him into a time the next day, Frank agrees to meet with him at 5:30.

- Is it ethical for Frank to see a client under these circumstances?
- If it *is* ethical, share your reasoning.
- If it *is not*, explain your position. If he breached the code of ethics that you are required to follow, describe all possible breaches with reference to the applicable section numbers within the standards of practice guidelines.
- What are some possible problems or risks with this plan?
- What should Frank do if the client will only agree to see him, and therefore will not go to the crisis clinic, yet still insists on being seen that day?
- If Frank refuses to see the client, is he being ethical?
- What might happen to their therapeutic relationship if Frank firmly tells the client that he will not see him on Wednesday and if he wants to be seen, the next available appointment is on Monday; and otherwise, he can use the crisis clinic?

My response:

14

Boris just picked up a new case through his private practice. The parents of a 13-year-old boy have asked Boris to see him to help him to "quit smoking pot." When he sees the boy privately for the first time, however, clearly the boy has no desire to quit or even cut down, but he does want help to sort through his feelings about his sexual orientation. His parents have no idea that he is questioning his sexuality, and he does not want them to know. Since it is the boy's parents who are paying the bill, Boris addresses their goal and uses motivational interviewing with their son to ease him toward the idea of quitting marijuana.

- Is Boris' decision ethical?
- If it *is*, explain why it is ethical.
- If it *is not*, explain your position. If he breached the code of ethics that you are required to follow, describe all possible breaches with reference to the applicable section numbers within the standards of practice guidelines.
- How do you determine who is the client?
- In what ways and to what extent will Boris' approach affect the youth? Do you think the boy will trust social workers or psychotherapists in the future? Why or why not?

My response:

15

Isabelle is a grant writer at a nonprofit grassroots agency. Sometimes she makes personal calls during her work day using the phone and phone line in her office, which is paid for by the agency and meant for business use only. She has never received explicit permission to do this, but she does not think her boss would mind.

- Is Isabelle acting unethically?
- If *no*, please explain your position.
- If *yes*, what is your reasoning? If she is breaching the code of ethics that you are required to follow, describe all possible breaches with reference to the applicable section numbers within the standards of practice guidelines.
- Would it make a difference if the calls were long distance? What if the calls were to a phone sex line?

My response:

16

Agostino is employed as a family mediator and has just completed a successful mediation of the separation of assets for a divorce proceeding that was quite bitter. A week after the final appointment, the wife involved in the mediation phones Agostino at his office and asks him out on a date, which he accepts.

- Would this behavior be considered ethical?
- If it *would be*, please share your reasoning.
- If it *would not be*, explain your position. If he breached the code of ethics that you are required to follow, describe all possible breaches with reference to the applicable section numbers within the standards of practice guidelines.
- Would it make a difference if the wife called him after the divorce was finalized? Why or why not? What if she asked him out ten years later?

My response:

17

Sooki works at a crisis pregnancy center that helps women who are pregnant find alternatives to abortion. She recently had a client who had already made up her mind that she wanted an abortion but asked Sooki to help her cope with the feelings of guilt that her decision was causing. The abortion was scheduled for the next week, and Sooki agreed to meet with her every other day until her appointment at the abortion clinic. It was Sooki's hope that she would be able to convince the client to have the baby and not abort it.

- Was it ethical for Sooki to behave like this?
- If it *was*, explain why it was ethical.
- If it *was not*, please justify your position. If she breached the code of ethics that you are required to follow, describe all possible breaches with reference to the applicable section numbers within the standards of practice guidelines.
- Under what circumstances is it justifiable to push or pull clients in a different direction for what you perceive to be their own good or the good of others?

My response:

18

Mabel is a group co-facilitator in a program that works with clients who have assertiveness issues. During one of the sessions, a female group member describes an incident in which she gave in to her teenage son's demands for money to go out with his friends, even though she could not afford it. In front of everyone, Mabel shouts at her, "Stop being such a wimp and stand up to him!"

- Is it unethical for Mabel to act in this manner?
- If *no*, please explain your reasoning.
- If *yes*, what exactly is unethical and why? If she breached the code of ethics that you are required to follow, describe all possible breaches with reference to the applicable section numbers within the standards of practice guidelines.
- What impact do you think this outburst would have on the client? What impact, if any, might it have on the other group members?
- What responsibility does Mabel's co-facilitator have in a situation like this one?

My response:

19

Tyrone is a fairly new social worker employed as a policy advisor with a municipal government. While going through some financial spreadsheets, he noticed some irregularities. Upon further investigation, he uncovered evidence that one of his co-workers, a non-social worker, had been falsifying the books and $2,000 appeared to be missing. Rather than report her to their supervisor, he spoke to her privately about his suspicions and sternly warned her that he will report her if it happens again. She denied any knowledge of fraudulent activity and refused to speak to or acknowledge him again, even though they work in the same office.

* Did Tyrone act ethically?
* If *yes*, please share your thoughts on why it was not unethical.
* If *no*, explain your reasoning. If he did breach the code of ethics that you are required to follow, describe all possible breaches with reference to the applicable section numbers within the standards of practice guidelines.
* Let's say Tyrone had decided to report her and she ended up getting fired and charged with fraud. How might this affect his relationships with the other office employees, especially given that she had worked there for years and was very well liked?

My response:

20

Kimberly provided family counseling to a mother and her two pre-teen sons for two months, and progress toward their goals was noticeable. It was close to the Christmas holidays, and at the end of one of their sessions, the mother presented Kim with a card and a gift certificate for $100. She accepted the gift with warm appreciation.

* Was it ethical of Kimberly to accept the gift?
* If it *was*, discuss your position.
* If it *was not* ethical, share your reasoning. If she breached the code of ethics that you are required to follow, describe all possible breaches with reference to the applicable section numbers within the standards of practice guidelines.
* Would it be ethical if she only accepted the card and gave back the gift certificate?
* What if the mother was very wealthy and could easily afford the $100?
* What if the mother lived paycheck to paycheck, yet insisted on Kim taking a *$1,000* gift certificate in appreciation of her service? Would it make a difference if, culturally, it would be an insult to the client and her family if Kimberly refused to accept the gift? Please share your thoughts.

My response:

21

Rael provides play therapy to children who have been sexually abused. During an individual session with a 4-year-old girl, while he was sitting cross-legged beside her, she came over and sat in his lap. Even though he was surprised and uncomfortable, he did not ask her to get off of him.

- Was Rael's lack of direction to the girl unethical?
- If he *was not* being unethical, explain your reasoning.
- If *he was*, discuss your position. If he breached the code of ethics that you are required to follow, describe all possible breaches with reference to the applicable section numbers within the standards of practice guidelines.
- Would your opinion change if the girl was 10 years old? What if it was a male child? If this situation was faced by a female social worker instead, would your reaction be the same?

My response:

22

Irina is a newly hired social worker at a smoke-free penitentiary. While walking across the yard, she is approached by one of the inmates who pleads with her to give him a cigarette. She feels sorry for him, but knows that it is against the rules. She decides to slip him one of her cigarettes when they shake hands good-bye.

- Is Irina's decision ethical?
- If it *is*, please explain your reasoning.
- If it *is not*, explain your position. If she breached the code of ethics that you are required to follow, describe all possible breaches with reference to the applicable section numbers within the standards of practice guidelines.
- How will she likely be perceived by at least this one inmate, if not all, once word gets around that she gives out cigarettes? What might this encourage?
- What impact might her decision have on her colleagues who hold the line firm?
- What could be the possible impact of her action on the tone of the prison and the ability of the staff to maintain authority?

My response:

May not be reproduced without permission of the publisher. Please use additional sheets if necessary.

23

Linda is supposed to work from 9 a.m. to 5 p.m. every weekday with a half-hour lunch and two 15-minute breaks. Her schedule is flexible and not monitored closely by management. At least three times per week, Linda takes extended lunches (1 to 1½ hours), and on most days she leaves at 4:30 p.m, after all of her work is done. She routinely signs the pay sheets as if she has been at work the whole time, according to the schedule.

- Are these behaviors ethical?
- If they *are* ethical, please discuss your position.
- If *no*, explain why not. If she is breaching the code of ethics that you are required to follow, describe all possible breaches with reference to the applicable section numbers within the standards of practice guidelines.
- Would it make an ethical difference if she took the day off and no one in administration noticed that she signed that she was there all day?

My response:

24

Danette, who works for Child Protective Services, recently investigated a case of alleged physical abuse of an 8-year-old boy who told a teacher that his father had hit him. The boy lives with his mother and father in a trailer park. There was no physical evidence of abuse and no witnesses to verify it. The neighbors, friends, and extended family had only positive things to say about the father and the family. The father denied ever physically abusing his son, and the boy's mother told Danette that her son was angry at his dad for sending him to bed early for cussing. She added that she thought he was lying, given that he had made up false allegations in the past. The boy eventually recanted his allegation. However, Danette did not like the father right away, because he reminded her of another father she had investigated recently from another trailer park who was very violent, alcoholic, and had a negative attitude. Without consulting her supervisor, she decided to remove the child from the home based on her belief that the boy had been beaten by his father and that he had recanted out of fear of retaliation. She was also convinced that the mother was covering up the abuse, which she believed may have been going on for years.

- Was it ethical for Danette to act in this manner?
- If *yes*, why?
- If *no*, explain your position. If Danette breached the code of ethics that you are required to follow, describe all possible breaches with reference to the applicable section numbers within the standards of practice guidelines.
- Who is Danette's client? What is her duty to the client? Does he/she/they/it have any say in what happens?
- Assuming the allegations are false, how might the boy feel? How might the father feel? How might the mother feel? How will this decision affect them as a family? Will this teach the boy a helpful lesson? Why or why not? Is this an abuse of power? Why or why not?

My response:

25

Jackie has many issues with distraction, concentration, and organization. Her desk is almost always scattered with papers. She is behind in much of her documentation and, admittedly, she does not record events in client files every time she is required to document. When she does write something, the notes are very brief and vague, mainly because she does not remember the details. She routinely back-dates the notes so she does not get in trouble with her boss.

- Would this behavior be considered ethical?
- If *yes*, explain your reasoning.
- If *no*, why is it not ethical? If Jackie is breaching the code of ethics that you are required to follow, describe all possible breaches with reference to the applicable section numbers within the standards of practice guidelines.
- List all the reasons you can think of for proper documentation.
- Who can or should she talk to about getting help for these issues?

My response:

26

Wendy has a private practice and sees her clients in a basement home office. She has a large family and, therefore, her washer and dryer in the basement laundry room are often in use while she sees clients. Sometimes she is in the middle of a session when the dryer buzzer loudly goes off, at which time she politely excuses herself while she changes over her laundry.

- Is Wendy's practice an ethical one?
- If it *is* ethical, what reasons would you give if you were to defend her?
- If it is *not*, what are the issues? If she breached the code of ethics that you are required to follow, describe all possible breaches with reference to the applicable section numbers within the standards of practice guidelines.
- What message(s) do you think this behavior sends to the clients? What do you think the clients might think and feel?

My response:

27

Xiu is a new social worker employed at a social welfare office. He met with a female Muslim client, and for the first time in his life, he was faced with someone wearing a niqāb, or full-faced veil. Because he is legally deaf, he needs to see the lips of those who speak to him to understand what they are saying. He, therefore, insisted that she uncover her face, stating that he could not and would not serve her unless she complied. She refused to reveal herself to him, and she would not leave. There were no other caseworkers available who could meet with her, because they all had left early for the long weekend. Xiu, being the new guy, had to stay and cover the desk the last half hour until the office closed. This woman refused, under any circumstances, to show her face to a man for religious and modesty reasons.

- Was it ethical for Xiu to act in this manner?
- If it *was*, please share your position.
- If it *was not* ethical, explain why it was not. If Xiu breached the code of ethics that you are required to follow, describe all possible breaches with reference to the applicable section numbers within the standards of practice guidelines.
- Who was being more unreasonable?
- Was there any discrimination shown here? If yes, by whom?
- What would you have done if you were Xiu?

My response:

28

Mary-Lou normally charges her private clients $120 for each 50-minute session, and the exchange of money is done at the end of the meeting. She sees a female client on an individual basis. As was arranged at the last session, the client brought along her husband and their three children for a family session. At the end of the session, Mary-Lou surprised them when she announced for the first time that she charges $150 for family sessions. The client and her husband were furious at her for this "bait and switch." They paid, but vowed never to seek services from a social worker again.

- Did Mary-Lou act in an ethical way?
- If she *was* being ethical, share your reasoning.
- If she *was not*, explain your position. If she breached the code of ethics that you are required to follow, describe all possible breaches with reference to the applicable section numbers within the standards of practice guidelines.
- Who was affected by these events?
- How could this misunderstanding have been prevented?

My response:

29

Amanda has received several past warnings by co-workers and supervisors that she needs to maintain her professional boundaries better with clients. She does not see an issue, however, strongly believing that it is important to be down-to-earth and genuine with clients, and that they need to be treated as human beings, not with a distant, cold, objective approach. Amanda does not like the idea of power imbalances, and instead, she wants equality in all of her relationships. When she develops close therapeutic bonds with clients, they feel like friendships to her. On several occasions, Amanda has given out her home phone number to clients, and she sends text messages to them regularly, both while at work and on her own time. Amanda stresses to her colleagues that these are platonic and therapeutic relationships only, and insists that the needs of her clients to have nonjudgmental and positive contact with a caring person like herself are her primary concern.

- Would Amanda's behavior be considered ethical?
- If *yes*, share your reasoning.
- If she *is not* being ethical, explain why not. If she is breaching the code of ethics that you are required to follow, describe all possible breaches with reference to the applicable section numbers within the standards of practice guidelines.
- If you were to defend her, what would you say about her approach?
- If you were to stand against her, perhaps as a manager, what issues of concern would you raise and why?

My response:

30

Iain is a social worker who likes to assess clients more thoroughly than his colleagues at the mental health clinic where he works. Without his supervisor's knowledge, he administers assessment tools that psychologists usually use, such as the MMPI. Then he gives the clients detailed feedback as to the interpretation of their individual scores. Iain typically provides them with one or more DSM diagnoses as well, even though he is not required to and none of his colleagues do it.

- Would Iain's behavior be considered ethical?
- If *yes*, it is ethical, please share your thoughts.
- If *no*, explain your position. If Iain breached the code of ethics that you are required to follow, describe all possible breaches with reference to the applicable section numbers within the standards of practice guidelines.
- Are there laws in your state or province that govern regulated professions and limit or restrict certain practices? If yes, did Iain contravene any statute?
- Do you think this practice leads to any confusion for the consumers? If yes, in what way(s)?

My response:

31

Lynne is a social worker in the health care field who recently earned a Ph.D. in human behavior through a six-month distance education program at an unaccredited school. For the past two months, she has been introducing herself as "Dr. Smith" and has ordered new business cards for herself with her new title.

- Is it ethical for Lynne to use this title?
- If *yes*, share your reasoning.
- If it *is not*, why not? If she breached the code of ethics that you are required to follow, describe all possible breaches with reference to the applicable section numbers within the standards of practice guidelines.
- Are there laws in your state or province that govern regulated professions and the use of titles? If so, did Lynne contravene any statute?

My response:

32

Vivian is a social worker at a residential program for pregnant teenagers. One of her clients is only 14 and very naïve. Because the client is so young, Vivian developed some treatment goals for her without her input and set up a program of activities and groups that she will need to attend to work toward these goals.

- Was it ethical for Vivian to act in this manner?
- If it *was*, please explain your position.
- If it *was not* ethical, what reason(s) would you give? If Vivian breached the code of ethics that you are required to follow, describe all possible breaches with reference to the applicable section numbers within the standards of practice guidelines.
- By residing in the program and attending the skills groups and activities, can it be assumed that the client is in agreement with the goals as designed by Vivian, which are basically the same for all the residents? Please explain.

My response:

33

Jeff met with a particularly attractive male client for the fourth time. He thought the client found him attractive, too, and they actively flirted with each other throughout their fourth meeting. Jeff left his office chair and sat beside the client on the couch. They started to kiss, which led to a sexual encounter.

- Did Jeff act ethically?
- If *yes*, explain your reasoning.
- If *not*, why not? If Jeff breached the code of ethics that you are required to follow, describe all possible breaches with reference to the applicable section numbers within the standards of practice guidelines.
- Would your opinion change if they decided to officially break off their professional relationship right after the encounter? Please explain.
- Would you still think the same way if they recinded their professional relationship right before Jeff sat down beside the client? Why or why not?
- What if they only kissed and did not have a sexual encounter? Would your opinion change?
- Would your opinion be different if the social worker and the client were of opposite sexes? Please explain.

My response:

34

Inga is employed by the federal government as a researcher in public health. She has had a fairly happy 15-year career in her position. But, over the past year, she has been bitter over several unwelcome changes, including some new "stupid" departmental policies and a new manager with whom she has not been getting along. When Inga found out that there would be major cuts in her department and that her job might be eliminated, she sent an e-mail to her manager. She copied the letter to several high ranking bureaucrats within the public health department. This letter bluntly expressed her unflattering opinion of the department, of the government, and of individual bureaucrats she worked under. She used extremely foul language with an intimidating tone. Inga ended the letter with a threat of what would happen to certain individuals if her job was taken from her.

- Would Inga's behavior be considered ethical?
- If *yes*, share your reasoning.
- If *no*, explain your position. If Inga breached the code of ethics that you are required to follow, describe all possible breaches with reference to the applicable section numbers within the standards of practice guidelines.
- What if she wrote the e-mail without the threat and sent it only to her manager, trusting that he would keep it private with the understanding that she was just "venting"? Does this change your mind? Why or why not?
- What might happen to such an e-mail sent to a supervisor? Are there different ethical implications based on what happens to it?

My response:

35

Zsuzsanna is a social worker at a long-term care facility. For the past five years, she has been a field instructor for social work students from a local university. This past term, she had an intern who did not show much drive or initiative. During supervision, when Zsuzsanna confronted her on her poor work ethic, the intern shared that she suffers from clinical depression and that it takes a lot of energy just to get out of bed in the morning, let alone do all the running around that is required of the field placement. The intern was unable to improve in the areas that were identified in time for the final evaluation, so Zsuzsanna was forced to give her a failing grade. The student burst out in tears when told of this decision, and she begged for a passing mark because she "could not possibly go through another 4-month placement" and she "just had to" graduate with her class in the spring. In desperation, the intern offered Zsuzsanna $900 in cash to change the report to a passing grade. Out of sympathy, and because she needed the money for a car repair, she accepted the offer with the confidence that no one would ever know.

- Was Zsuzsanna's decision ethical?
- If it *was*, please explain your reasoning.
- If it *was not*, please share your thoughts. If she breached the code of ethics that you are required to follow, describe all possible breaches with reference to the applicable section numbers within the standards of practice guidelines.
- Would it have been ethical if Zsuzsanna had decided to change the grade based on the pleading and tears alone, without the bribe? Please explain.
- If the intern's poor performance was due to a verifiable mental illness, which could be considered a disability, would it be fair (or even legal) to judge her according to the same standards that would be applied to a non-disabled person? Share your thoughts.

My response:

36

Julio just wrapped up his final session with an adult female client. She was at the doorway to go when she asked for a good-bye hug from him. Julio hesitated, and then hugged her as she hugged him. She then walked out the door.

- Would this behavior be considered ethical?
- If *yes*, explain why.
- If *no*, share your position. If Julio breached the code of ethics that you are required to follow, describe all possible breaches with reference to the applicable section numbers within the standards of practice guidelines.
- What if the hug included a two-cheek kiss, customary in some cultures? If this changes your opinion, please explain.
- What if the hug included a peck on the lips? If this changes your opinion, please explain.
- What if the kiss involved the tongue? If this changes your opinion, please explain.
- If he purposely touched her buttocks with his hand during the hug, would this change your opinion? Please explain. What if his hand was placed on her hip instead?

My response:

37

Scarlett has a new client with a significant trauma history. The client wants to address her past to stop her flashbacks. Scarlett has no previous experience in trauma work and has never attended any training on it, nor has she completed any reading on the subject. She figures that the best way to learn is by doing, so she contracts with this client for service.

- Is Scarlett acting ethically?
- If she *is*, please explain your reasoning.
- If the answer is *no*, why is she not? If she breached the code of ethics that you are required to follow, describe all possible breaches with reference to the applicable section numbers within the standards of practice guidelines.
- What are some of the possible consequences should Scarlett work with this client?
- Would your mind change if Scarlett had a supervisor who is an expert in trauma, who can meet with her between sessions? Please explain.

My response:

38

Ahmed worked with a wealthy 85-year-old woman through a drop-in center for seniors who suffer from cognitive deficits, many with early dementia. He gained the trust of this woman, and she sometimes called him her grandson, even though he clearly was not. They met privately every day, and during this time, Ahmed routinely steered the conversation toward her will, asking how much money and property she had, and who was named in her will. Over time, he pressured her to name him as the sole beneficiary of her estate. She finally did this through her lawyer, who did not suspect that her capacity in such matters was impaired.

- Could Ahmed's behavior be considered ethical?
- If it *could be* ethical, please share your reasoning.
- If it clearly *is not* ethical, explain why not. If Ahmed breached the code of ethics that you are required to follow, describe all possible breaches with reference to the applicable section numbers within the standards of practice guidelines.
- If the client had previously appointed a continuing power of attorney, could this have helped? Please explain.

My response:

39

Julie provided marriage counseling to a man and a woman who had been married for three years but bickered and argued frequently, and could not agree on a parenting plan for their 2-year-old son. Julie shared with the couple that she and her husband had similar difficulties early in their marriage as well, especially around the issue of parenting. She went on to tell them what seemed to help and what did not help for them, going into some detail about their past struggles.

- Would this behavior be considered ethical?
- If *yes*, explain your position.
- If *no*, what is your reasoning? If Julie breached the code of ethics that you are required to follow, describe all possible breaches with reference to the applicable section numbers within the standards of practice guidelines.
- How much self disclosure is too much? What would it look like if there was absolutely none?

My response:

40

Savinna works at a secular family counseling center and has very strong Christian values, which she draws from in her work with families. She frequently prays with her clients without invitation. At other times, she will give a mini-sermon about Jesus, His sacrifice for our sins, and the need to live a pure and Christian lifestyle. She also speaks of going to hell for breaking His commandments, and she is noticeably cold toward clients who have committed adultery or appear to her to be gay.

- Is this ethical behavior?
- If *yes*, share your position.
- If *no*, explain your reasoning. If she breached the code of ethics that you are required to follow, describe all possible breaches with reference to the applicable section numbers within the standards of practice guidelines.
- How might clients feel if they do not share her religion or her version of Christianity, yet Savinna acts in these ways? Even if they do share these beliefs, what might they think of the practice of social work?

My response:

41

Ashley is a social worker at a youth shelter. A teen-age girl whom she has known for almost a year came to her office, once again complaining of suicidal ideation. As usual, she had fresh superficial scratches on her arms. The youth said she was going to cut her arms really deep this time and hoped to "bleed out." Ashley knows this girl well and her theatrics have become tiresome, as she has made similar threats without incident several dozen times since Ashley first met her. Ashley decided to use "reverse psychology" and told the teen that she was right, that she probably should kill herself.

- Was Ashley's decision ethical?
- If *yes*, please describe your reasoning.
- If *no*, explain your position. If she breached the code of ethics that you are required to follow, describe all possible breaches with reference to the applicable section numbers within the standards of practice guidelines.
- What do you think the client might think and feel as a result of what Ashley said to her? Do you think her risk of suicide would go up, down, or stay the same in this scenario?

My response:

42

Gina is a social worker in private practice and sees several clients each day for general counseling. Her office where she meets with clients is decorated with posters, pins, banners, signs, and drink coasters, all with political slogans and logos for her political party and for the candidate she supports for an upcoming election.

*   Is it ethical to have an office decorated like Gina's?
*   If *yes*, why is it ethical?
*   If *no*, explain your reasoning. If she breached the code of ethics that you are required to follow, describe all possible breaches with reference to the applicable section numbers within the standards of practice guidelines.
*   Would your opinion change if she only had a framed photograph on her office wall of her and the easily recognizable candidate standing together?
*   Would it make a difference if she were employed by an agency (public or private) rather than in private practice?
*   At what point, if at all, does or should Gina's right to freedom of speech and freedom of expression get restricted by professional ethics? Please share your thoughts.

My response:

43

Marcel is a 67-year-old social worker called back from retirement on a temporary contract to manage a program that he helped to develop and that he ran until retiring two years ago. Since returning to work last month, he has found that he is forgetting to do very important tasks and has missed key meetings with stakeholders. Marcel missed the deadline for payroll to go in, and he recently got lost in the office building that he used to know so well. Most of the day, he is lost in confusion, trying to find important files that he set down somewhere. Marcel plugs along, not wanting to disappoint anyone and with the hope that things will improve once he gets his bearings.

- Is it ethical for Marcel to continue working under these circumstances?
- If *yes*, please share your position.
- If *no*, explain your reasoning. If he is breaching the code of ethics that you are required to follow, describe all possible breaches with reference to the applicable section numbers within the standards of practice guidelines.
- What would you do if you were Marcel? What would you do if you were the executive director of the agency who hired him? What would you do if you had to work under Marcel?

My response:

44

Colleen is a functional alcoholic, although she will not admit that she has a problem with drinking. She has never missed a day of work at the children's hospital, where she provides social work services to the children and their families. She has, however, come to work still intoxicated from drinking the night before her morning shift. On these days, Colleen tries to isolate herself in her office and do paperwork until she sobers up.

- Would this behavior be considered ethical?
- If it *is* ethical, what are the reasons?
- If it *is not*, please share your thoughts. If Colleen breached the code of ethics that you are required to follow, describe all possible breaches with reference to the applicable section numbers within the standards of practice guidelines.
- What problems could this behavior lead to? What is Colleen risking?

My response:

45

Brandon is a group facilitator for a court mandated, psychoedu-cational group for men who have been physically abusive toward their intimate partners. He generally does not know who will be in his group until their first day, since it is the coordinator of the pro-gram who does the orientation and screening of new members, who then are assigned a start date. On one of the start days, Brandon is surprised to find his own brother sitting in the group. Brandon feels very uncomfortable with the prospect of facilitating a group with his brother in it and asks to speak with his brother privately in the hallway. The brother pleads to be allowed to stay, saying that he will go to jail if he does not start the group that day, as he has missed three other start dates already. Brandon agrees to let him stay.

- Is it ethical for Brandon to provide services to his brother?
- If *yes*, share your opinion.
- If *no*, what are your reasons? If he breached the code of ethics that you are required to follow, describe all possible breaches with reference to the applicable section numbers within the standards of practice guidelines.
- Would it have been ethical to deny his brother the service that would prevent him from going to jail, especially since he was at the group on time, cooperative, and willing to work? Why or why not?

My response:

46

Cathy is a social worker who works in an office environment as a case manager. Her friends and colleagues would agree that she is very social, "bubbly," and fun to be around. She is usually very funny and often uses sexual innuendo, especially around male colleagues. One morning, she entered the photocopy room where a good looking man who was fairly new in the office was finishing up a job. She playfully came up to him, grabbed his left buttock, and in an exaggerated sexy voice asked, "Do you want to get lucky?"

- Is this ethical behavior?
- If *yes*, explain how it is ethical.
- If *no*, share your thoughts. If Cathy breached the code of ethics that you are required to follow, describe all possible breaches with reference to the applicable section numbers within the standards of practice guidelines.
- How do you think this man might have felt? Do you think the feelings would be different if Cathy did this to a woman? How about if a man was doing it to a woman? Or perhaps a man to a man? Please share your thoughts.

My response:

May not be reproduced without permission of the publisher. Please use additional sheets if necessary.

47

Natalia is a registered social worker and needs to renew her professional license on an annual basis. On the renewal form is a section that asks if she has been convicted of a criminal offense or investigated for a criminal offense since she last renewed. Natalia was, in fact, convicted of possessing a small amount of marijuana for personal use six months earlier, but has already completed her sentence of community service and a fine. She considers the embarrassing affair over and done with, and she checks the "No" box before signing and sending in the form with her annual payment.

- Was Natalia's decision ethical?
- If it *was* ethical, describe your reasoning.
- If it *was not*, why not? If she breached the code of ethics that you are required to follow, describe all possible breaches with reference to the applicable section numbers within the standards of practice guidelines.
- Why should Natalia admit to something so small that will likely never get checked, which potentially could put her whole career on hold, and possibly lead to her losing her job if she cannot re-register?

My response:

48

Yoshi is an addictions worker at a residential treatment center. He just received a phone call from the mother of one of his young adult clients. She said that while her son was on a pass with her earlier in the day, she saw him take some unidentified pills. When she challenged him, he denied taking anything. Yoshi immediately called the client in question into his office and confronted him on what his mother had said. The client became enraged, claiming that Yoshi had breached confidentiality.

• Did Yoshi behave unethically?
• If *no*, explain your reasoning.
• If *yes*, in what way(s)? If he did breach the code of ethics that you are required to follow, describe all possible breaches with reference to the applicable section numbers within the standards of practice guidelines.
• What, if any, rules were broken according to the privacy legislation that you are required to follow? What can you receive from whom, and what can you share with whom, without expressed consent of the client?

My response:

May not be reproduced without permission of the publisher. Please use additional sheets if necessary.

49

Martin and one of his best friends are both employed with an assertive community treatment team. At the water cooler, Martin tells his friend a story about one of their shared clients with a mental illness who one day stripped naked, climbed a communications tower, and urinated off of it. Both of them began laughing loudly, making fun of the client, and commenting on how crazy the client appeared that night.

- Would this behavior be considered ethical?
- If *yes*, explain your reasoning.
- If *no*, what is your position? If the code of ethics that you are required to follow was breached here, describe all possible breaches with reference to the applicable section numbers within the standards of practice guidelines.
- If you said it was ethical, at what point would it become unethical? Use the scenario above to write further and give examples of what might be said that you think would "cross the line."
- If you said it was unethical, at what point did the story, as told above, become unethical? Fill in the details, line-by-line, of what might have been said between the two friends and identify the point at which it became unethical.

My response:

50

Gisele is a social worker at a busy hospital, and she often needs to discuss cases with doctors and other staff while walking from one place to another within the building. While in an elevator that contained several other people not involved in the case, she openly talked about a patient's discharge needs with the doctor, but was careful not to mention the person's name.

- Is this unethical behavior?
- If it *is not*, explain why.
- If it *is* unethical, share your thoughts. If Gisele did breach the code of ethics that you are required to follow, describe all possible breaches with reference to the applicable section numbers within the standards of practice guidelines.
- Imagine why others might disagree with your opinion. What might be their argument?
- What are the consequences for breaching confidentiality, according to the privacy legislation that you are required to follow?

My response:

51

Tracy works in a residential program for behaviorally challenged youth. On a camping trip with the clients, Tracy was assigned by the supervisor to a 5-person tent with four girls between the ages of 10 and 14. On the evening of the second day, the group of 15 residents and four staff were sitting around the campfire when a 12-year-old from Tracy's tent said that she was not feeling well and went to lie down in the tent. A few minutes later, Tracy went to check on her. The client was sitting up in her sleeping bag and complained that she had a bad headache and her neck and back muscles were really tight. Tracy offered to give her a back massage, which was accepted. There were no witnesses.

- Was Tracy acting in an ethical manner?
- If it was *ethical*, explain your reasoning.
- If she was acting *unethically*, please explain your position. If she breached the code of ethics that you are required to follow, describe all possible breaches with reference to the applicable section numbers within the standards of practice guidelines.
- If you decided Tracy was behaving ethically, would it have made a difference if a male staff member had massaged the 12-year-old girl's back alone in the tent? What if the male staff was openly gay? Is it reasonable to determine ethics by gender or sexual orientation?
- If you decided that she was acting unethically, what would you have done differently?

My response:

52

Sergio is the clinical director of a four- to six-month-long residential drug treatment program for federal parolees. Residents are expected to remain drug free, follow the center's rules, and participate in all aspects of programming as a condition of their parole. Those who are unable to follow these expectations are unceremoniously re-arrested and transported back to prison. Francis is a resident who knows he has used all of his chances, but he has made progress in his therapy and has otherwise been an average resident. After the weekly team meeting during which they discussed his fate, Francis went directly to Sergio to find out if they talked about him. Sergio lied to the client, and said that a decision had not been made yet, when in fact the team unanimously had agreed that the center should revoke support of his parole. The call to the police had already been made. Sergio further misled Francis by inviting him for a walk on the grounds to discuss his progress in treatment, when his true agenda was to get Francis outside and away from the other residents when they met the police cruiser. Sergio felt uneasy about the deception, but on a few occasions in the past when residents had been informed ahead of time that they were going back to prison, they had acted out violently and/or tried to escape. Sergio did not want to take that risk with Francis.

- Was Sergio's deception ethical?
- If it *was*, describe your reasoning.
- If it *was not*, why not? If he breached the code of ethics that you are required to follow, describe all possible breaches with reference to the applicable section numbers within the standards of practice guidelines.
- Who was the client in this case—the resident, the parole board that permitted him to attend the treatment center, or the parole office supervising his conditional release? Should Sergio's loyalty be to the residents or to the legal system?
- What would you have done if you were in Sergio's position?

My response:

May not be reproduced without permission of the publisher. Please use additional sheets if necessary.

53

Jo Anne runs an after-school program to help keep kids off the street and away from gangs. After she did a talk on healthy sexuality with a small group of 12- and 13-year-old girls, one of the girls asked to talk to her in private. She disclosed to Jo Anne that a couple of days earlier, a "creepy" neighbor had come up to her when she was alone outside walking her dog, and flashed his privates at her. The girl said that she had told her parents right away and they had called the police. Jo Anne provided the girl with support and reassurance, but decided against calling the police or child protective services herself, taking the girl at her word that her parents had called the police. She assumed that the police would have automatically notified the child protection agency to join in the investigation. Jo Anne did not follow up by speaking to the girl's parents and never made her own report to the police or any other agency. She did not mention it to her manager and wrote no report of her own.

- Were Jo Anne's decisions ethical?
- If they *were*, please explain why.
- If they *were not*, share your thoughts. If Jo Anne breached the code of ethics that you are required to follow, describe all possible breaches with reference to the applicable section numbers within the standards of practice guidelines.
- Are there additional state or provincial laws that you are required to follow when child protection is an issue? If so, would they apply in this case?
- What are the implications if it turns out that the girl never told her parents, or if she did, that no action was taken on their end, and the neighbor escalates his sexually aggressive behavior?

My response:

54

Laughlin is a social worker who just overheard that he is going to be investigated by his employer and the police for allegations against him of inappropriate sexual touching and extortion of a current client of his at an HIV clinic. His licensing board will most likely be called in very shortly, as well. Laughlin is responsible for all that was alleged and he immediately calls the client to plead for her to recant her allegations, but she refuses. He decides to remove her file from the main reception area and impulsively shreds all of it, thinking that it might contain evidence that can be used against him, perhaps from others on the multidisciplinary team if she has told them. Out of desperation, he decides to go to the client's house to confront her. He keeps a knife in his car.

- Is this unethical behavior?
- If *no*, explain why not.
- If *yes*, share your reasons. If Laughlin did breach the code of ethics that you are required to follow, describe all possible breaches with reference to the applicable section numbers within the standards of practice guidelines.
- How can employers identify troubled employees and work with them to prevent such potentially tragic situations?
- What responsibility do faculty members and field instructors have when teaching or supervising social work students who present with significant character flaws or antisocial personality?

My response:

May not be reproduced without permission of the publisher. Please use additional sheets if necessary.

55

Daniel is a social worker who graduated four months ago and is in his first job counseling college students on stress management, exam anxiety, study tips, and other issues. In working with his first client, an 18-year-old male, they have developed goals around better managing the student's time so he can balance his social life with his school work. To date, the sessions have been spent talking the whole time about sports, music, and current events. In supervision, Daniel reports that he is building a very positive therapeutic rapport with his client and that things are going well.

- Is Daniel being ethical?
- If he *is*, share your reasoning.
- If he *is not* being ethical, explain why not. If he is breaching the code of ethics that you are required to follow, describe all possible breaches with reference to the applicable section numbers within the standards of practice guidelines.
- What might be behind Daniel's avoidance with his client and the deception with his supervisor?
- Why might the client be colluding with Daniel and not challenging him to be an effective counselor?

My response:

56

Pamela works at a hospital and is set to retire in 195 days. Emotionally, she is already semi-retired, putting half the effort into work that she used to enjoy. Now her colleagues just annoy her, and she is often short and curt with patients, showing little warmth or compassion. She can't wait for each day to end. It is not very pleasant to be around her, as she is very pessimistic when discussing her cases, and her comments are often passive-aggressive. Her colleagues have complained to management about how toxic she has become to the team, but they clearly are waiting her out until she retires.

- Is Pamela engaging in unethical behavior?
- If her behavior is *ethical*, please explain.
- If it is *unethical*, share your thoughts. If Pamela did breach the code of ethics that you are required to follow, describe all possible breaches with reference to the applicable section numbers within the standards of practice guidelines.
- Is there anything that the employer can do or provide that will improve the situation?
- What impact do you think her behavior has on her patients, both short- and long-term?

My response:

57

Stephanie works at a Veterans Administration hospital and discovers that one of her patients will not qualify for a new program that could really help him, because he was born one year too late. When she submits the referral, she changes the last digit of his year of birth from a "2" to a "1" on all of the paperwork, including past records that she was required to submit along with the application.

- Was Stephanie's deception ethical?
- If it *was*, describe your reasoning.
- If it *was not*, why not? If she breached the code of ethics that you are required to follow, describe all possible breaches with reference to the applicable section numbers within the standards of practice guidelines.
- When the intent is good, and the client's needs are clearly considered first, is it possible for an action to be unethical? Why or why not?
- When dealing with rigid, bureaucratic systems, is it not the norm to "work" the system so clients get what they need? Please discuss.

My response:

58

Meghan works for an agency that specializes in working with survivors of sexual assault. A young woman was referred to Meghan's agency by a social worker in private practice, because he did not feel equipped to deal with the issues of sexual abuse when they came up and seemed to block progress on the client's other goals. The social worker decided to keep an open file until the client returned to his private practice at the end of her sexual assault treatment. With signed consent, the male social worker sent Meghan his assessment report on the young woman, which had a blunt, but honest, formulation on the issues as he saw them. During a session with Meghan, the client requested to see her agency file, which was granted immediately. The client read the private practitioner's report without much reaction. A week later, the client quit her sessions at the agency and booked an appointment with the private social worker. When they met, she exploded with fury over how she was characterized in the formulation. Over the next half hour, they repaired their relationship enough to contract for further service. The private practitioner called Meghan, stating that she should have set aside reports from other professionals so these individuals could go over them with the client themselves to provide context and answer questions, preventing misinterpretation or misunderstanding. Meghan felt no regret, stating that clients are permitted to see their whole files at any time, with no limits.

- Which social worker is on the higher ethical ground?
- If the *private practitioner* is, share your reasoning.
- If it is the *agency social worker*, explain why.
- If either of them breached the code of ethics that you are required to follow, describe all possible breaches with reference to the applicable section numbers within the standards of practice guidelines.
- Do you think the private practitioner will think twice before volunteering to share written records with another agency? What are the potential implications?
- Can you think of any solutions to this dilemma?

My response:

May not be reproduced without permission of the publisher. Please use additional sheets if necessary.

59

Mustafa is a high school social worker and has always had to deal with uncomfortable phone calls from parents. Over the past two weeks, he has had a number of very challenging calls from one particular mother, who complains about petty issues, puts down her child's teachers, and makes her child out to be perfect. The calls are even more irritating because she will not give him a word in edgewise, and she is very difficult to get off the phone. At least 30 minutes per day is spent listening to her gripe. Mustafa has a caller ID display feature on his office phone, and since Monday, he has not been picking up her calls, so she has been getting his voicemail only. The messages from her have routinely been five minutes long (the maximum time possible), and Mustafa now deletes the messages without listening to them.

- Is Mustafa being ethical?
- If he *is*, explain your reasoning.
- If he *is not* being ethical, explain why not. If he is breaching the code of ethics that you are required to follow, describe all possible breaches with reference to the applicable section numbers within the standards of practice guidelines.
- What impact will his behavior have on the mother, for good or bad? If she does not feel heard, what might happen?
- If his client is the student, does he really need to deal with the mother? Why or why not?

My response:

60

Eva is a retired social worker who is still licensed. She spends much of her time as a social activist and recently organized a large protest at the State Capitol in response to a government plan to cut welfare payments. At her encouragement, a large group of protesters stormed the building and held a two-day sit-in on the floor of the legislative assembly. As a result of her actions, she was arrested by the police and charged with trespassing, causing a disturbance, resisting arrest, and obstruction of justice.

- Was Eva acting in an ethical manner?
- If it was *ethical*, explain your reasoning.
- If she was acting *unethically*, please explain your position. If Eva breached the code of ethics that you are required to follow, describe all possible breaches with reference to the applicable section numbers within the standards of practice guidelines.
- If you thought Eva acted ethically from the description above, at what point can grassroots political protest become unethical?
- If you thought her behavior was unethical, where was "the line" crossed?

My response:

61

Nicole works on a busy acquired brain injury unit. She took one of her female patients, a frail 62-year-old treatment capable and voluntary inpatient, out for a walk on the hospital grounds. As they were walking around the block on the perimeter of the property, her patient kept on walking across the quiet road to the next block. Nicole used all of the verbal skills that she could think of to encourage the patient to return to the hospital with her, but there was no response. She decided to take the patient by the arm and physically direct her back to the hospital without her consent.

- Was it ethical for Nicole to act in this way?
- If it *was*, explain your reasoning.
- If it *was not*, why not? If Nicole did breach the code of ethics that you are required to follow, describe all possible breaches with reference to the applicable section numbers within the standards of practice guidelines.
- What other options might Nicole have had in this situation?
- What possible consequences might Nicole face for this decision? What might have happened to her and the patient if she let the patient go missing? What possible consequences might she face for the decision that she made?
- What would you have done? Why?

My response:

62

Richard is a social worker in a municipal public housing department that provides advocacy, mental health support, and mediation between tenants in the subsidized housing units run by the city. He returned to his office after spending most of his morning meeting with a tenant who had a complaint about his neighbors above him spying on him and reading his mind. Richard asked the tenant to sign a release of information form to allow him to consult with the man's outpatient psychiatric team. Back at his office, it occurred to Richard that before the form was signed, he should have added to it that permission is given for him to consult with the man's family doctor, as well. Rather than return to the building to get a new form signed, Richard decided that he would just add to the existing signed form, as it was something that he had told the man would be a good idea.

- Was Richard's decision ethical?
- If it *was*, please explain why.
- If it *was not*, share your thoughts. If Richard breached the code of ethics that you are required to follow, describe all possible breaches with reference to the applicable section numbers within the standards of practice guidelines.
- If Richard was ever brought to court and this addition was the focus of the prosecutor's attention, what are the possible consequences for his behavior?
- If this happened in your region, and if the regulatory body that licenses social workers determined that Richard was guilty of a breach of ethics, what are the possible consequences? Please list all possibilities.

My response:

63

Cassandra is a social worker in private practice. Her husband is interested in hearing about her work and often asks about her day, wanting to hear some details. One night, while they are lying in bed talking about the next day, she confides that she is not looking forward to her upcoming 9 a.m. session because it is with a very obnoxious man. Perhaps it is because she is tired, or perhaps she knows her husband can keep a secret, but she ends up sharing personal information about her client with him, which leads him to ask more questions.

- Is Cassandra acting in an ethical manner?
- If it *is* ethical, explain your reasoning.
- If she is acting *unethically,* please explain your position. If she breached the code of ethics that you are required to follow, describe all possible breaches with reference to the applicable section numbers within the standards of practice guidelines.
- If you are responsible to uphold a privacy act in your state or province, does it cover what just happened with Cassandra? If so, which section(s)?
- If you thought that Cassandra was maintaining ethics, at what point would she "cross the line"? If you are sure that she did breach ethical standards in the above scenario, would it make a difference if she made sure not to share the client's name with her husband?

My response:

64

Guy works with a mental health team that provides short-term follow-up after discharge from the hospital. One of his clients, who is at the end of the three-month service, asks Guy for a referral to someone who provides similar services, but on a private basis. He decides to refer the client to his best friend from the university, who graduated with Guy from social work school 20 years ago. Guy considers the man to be a good friend, but has no firsthand knowledge of his skills as a social worker.

- Is Guy acting in an ethical manner?
- If his actions are *ethical*, explain your reasoning.
- If he is acting *unethically*, please explain your position. If he breached the code of ethics that you are required to follow, describe all possible breaches with reference to the applicable section numbers within the standards of practice guidelines.
- Do you think that Guy could be held responsible if his friend turns out to be unethical, incompetent, or in some way hurtful to the client?
- Is it a conflict of interest to refer someone to a friend?

My response:

65

Shaniqua works for a community-based nonprofit agency that advocates for low- and moderate-income families regarding a range of social issues. She needs to give an update to a client who is struggling with finding affordable housing. Shaniqua dials the number her client gave her, but it immediately goes to voicemail with only a "beep" sound, which did not happen the last time she called. She decides to leave a detailed, confidential message on the voicemail because it is the only way to get hold of her client.

- Did Shaniqua make an ethical decision?
- If you believe she *did* act ethically, what convinced you?
- If she *did not* act ethically, please explain your position. If she breached the code of ethics that you are required to follow, describe all possible breaches with reference to the applicable section numbers within the standards of practice guidelines.
- What are some possible consequences of her actions? Did she have other options?
- What would you have done if you were Shaniqua?

My response:

66

Raymond agrees to do some personal shopping for a cancer patient who has been hospitalized at the cancer treatment center for several weeks. Unfortunately, the patient is estranged from his family and no longer has any friends who can bring him some of the hygiene products and snacks that the hospital does not provide. Raymond goes by himself to the local department store to pick up items on a list provided by the patient. While at the store, he decides to spend an additional half-hour to do some personal shopping for himself, which he is careful to pay for separately. Raymond then drives the hospital minivan to his nearby home to drop off his purchases before heading back to work.

- Is Raymond engaging in unethical behavior?
- If his behavior *is* ethical, please explain.
- If it *is not*, share your position. If he breached the code of ethics that you are required to follow, describe all possible breaches with reference to the applicable section numbers within the standards of practice guidelines.
- Now take the opposite position and describe why others might disagree with your original decision.

My response:

67

Dana is a social worker who coordinates hearing dates and times for a review board panel that comes to her psychiatric hospital when necessary. The purpose of the panel is to hear patient appeals to psychiatrists' findings that they are incapable of managing their finances, incapable of making their own treatment decisions, or incapable of deciding to leave the hospital voluntarily, due to risk of harm to self or others. She recently arranged a review board hearing for a patient who wanted to appeal an involuntary status certificate that he was placed on by the psychiatrist, Dr. Hamilton. Dana is good friends with Dr. Hamilton and is aware that she has been struggling financially since the break-up with her husband. It is well known within the system that if a hearing is cancelled with less than 12 hours notice, all parties to the hearing (other than the patient), including the panel members, the lawyer(s), and the doctor, get paid for their time as if the hearing took place. Two days prior to the planned hearing, Dr. Hamilton removed the certificate on the patient, which gave him a voluntary status. Dr. Hamilton notified Dana of the need to cancel the hearing on that day. Unbeknownst to the doctor, Dana waited until the deadline had passed before calling in the cancellation, which ended up benefitting her friend financially.

- Was Dana acting in an ethical manner?
- If she acted *ethically*, please share your reasoning.
- If she acted *unethically*, what evidence do you have? If she breached the code of ethics that you are required to follow, describe all possible breaches with reference to the applicable section numbers within the standards of practice guidelines.
- How might this behavior affect the relationship between Dana and Dr. Hamilton? Could this place Dr. Hamilton at risk ethically? If so, how?

My response:

68

Phuong works for a small, nonprofit counseling agency that does not have very clear or detailed policies on many things, including documentation. Client files are simple file folders with a few loose papers in them, including a face sheet and a check box assessment. After a day of seeing clients, Phuong types each case note in about 3-4 lines, dates them with the month and day only, and then types his first name at the bottom of each small note. After printing the page, he cuts the notes out into individual strips and files them in each client folder without signing or initialing them. The program manager is his supervisor, and she is not a regulated professional. She does not have a concern with Phuong's documentation practice.

- Would Phuong's documentation be considered ethical?
- If it is *ethical*, please explain your thoughts.
- If it is *unethical*, what are your concerns? List any problems you notice in Phuong's practice and explain why. If he is breaching the code of ethics that you are required to follow, describe all possible breaches with reference to the applicable section numbers within the standards of practice guidelines.
- If an agency does not require its social workers to keep formal records, why should they do all that extra work?
- Why should an agency set and maintain documentation standards for its staff?

My response:

69

Brittany, a social worker at an outpatient methadone clinic, enjoys helping out in different areas when nursing staff call in sick or go on vacation. She works closely with several nurses who take blood and urine for lab tests, assess the stability of the clients, check for side effects, and give out methadone to the patients. Brittany has worked at the clinic for 15 years, and over time, her job role has slowly merged with the nurses' to the point that she has dispensed the methadone on occasion, and at other times, she has provided informal instruction to nursing students on how to properly landmark the arm for needle insertion to draw blood.

- Is Brittany acting in an ethical manner?
- If it is *ethical*, explain your reasoning.
- If she is acting *unethically*, please explain your position. If she breached the code of ethics that you are required to follow, describe all possible breaches with reference to the applicable section numbers within the standards of practice guidelines.
- What are some potential problems with Brittany's approach?
- Brittany's supervisor is a nurse, and they are good friends. What role should her supervisor play in this situation and why? What could happen if a supervisor is "too close" to his or her supervisees?

My response:

70

Donna is a resource coordinator for female victims of domestic violence through an agency that provides group intervention for men convicted of abusing these same partners. The contract the agency has with the government for the treatment of these mandated clients states that a resource coordinator must make contact or attempt to make contact with each victim at least four times during the 16-week program for the men. The women are not enrolled as clients with the agency, and as a result, they do not have official files. Donna is concerned, however, that if she puts her case notes from her contact with the women in the agency files of the male partners, then the men could have access to these notes if they request to review their files. Her solution is to keep the notes in an unsealed envelope clipped to the inside of each man's file.

- Is Donna's solution ethical?
- If it *is*, please explain why.
- If it *is not*, share your thoughts. If Donna breached the code of ethics that you are required to follow, describe all possible breaches with reference to the applicable section numbers within the standards of practice guidelines.
- How would you resolve this dilemma?

My response:

71

Chad is a school social worker who has learned that a 16-year-old pop star, who has become a teen idol and international media sensation, was previously a student at one of the schools that he covers. This boy was never actually a client of his, and he only learned of his name last year, when he started hearing it on the news and, later, on national talk shows. It is common for Chad to be in the file rooms in the various schools that he covers, but he made a special trip to the school that the boy attended up until last year, to see if the file was still there. It was, and he could not help himself—he just had to take a look. Flipping through the student file, he did not see anything too exciting, but did come across a psychological consultation report. It was like gold in his hands. Looking around, he saw no other staff around, so he quickly and nervously photocopied the report and then shoved it in his satchel before he was seen by other staff.

- Did Chad engage in unethical behavior?
- If his behavior was *ethical*, please explain why.
- If it was *unethical*, share your position. If Chad breached the code of ethics that you are required to follow, describe all possible breaches with reference to the applicable section numbers within the standards of practice guidelines.
- What might have happened to him if caught?
- In what ways could Chad benefit if he shared this information with others?
- What impact might this have on the teen star and his career? How might this boy feel?

My response:

72

Laurel is a fairly new graduate, eight months into her first social work job as a child and family counselor at a nonprofit agency. She has a 14-year-old female client with whom she is becoming increasingly frustrated. During the last three sessions the girl has called Laurel "stupid," a "lesbo," and has refused to talk about things that she openly spoke about with Laurel only a month ago. Laurel cannot figure out what is going on and the client will not tell her, although she is clearly dropping hints that she is unhappy about something. Laurel's supervisor meets with her weekly to discuss her cases, help resolve any difficulties she is having, and to share in her successes. Despite his openness, Laurel will not raise the above issue with her supervisor.

- Is Laurel acting in an ethical manner?
- If her behavior is *ethical*, what convinced you?
- If she is acting *unethically*, please explain your position. If she is breaching the code of ethics that you are required to follow, describe all possible breaches with reference to the applicable section numbers within the standards of practice guidelines.
- Why do you think Laurel is resistant to sharing the problem with her supervisor?
- What would you do if you were Laurel?

My response:

73

Fernando provides crisis assessments at a walk-in clinic. One evening a 15-year-old girl was brought to the clinic by a friend, and Fernando saw her alone. Her presenting concerns were depressed mood, feelings of hopelessness, and thoughts of suicide. She admitted to having intent to kill herself, but not immediately. On further questioning, she admitted to having a large bottle full of assorted prescription pills in her pocket. Fernando skillfully convinced the client to show him the pills. When he asked her to hand them over, she refused, however, clenching the bottle with both hands. Fernando stood up, and the teenager reacted by holding the bottle close to her chest. Recognizing the importance of separating the client from the intended means to kill herself, Fernando decided to wrestle her for the bottle of pills. He got bruised, and she received scratches during the struggle, and he accidentally touched her breast.

- Did Fernando make an ethical decision?
- If you believe he *did* act ethically, what convinced you?
- If he *did not* act ethically, please explain why not. If he breached the code of ethics that you are required to follow, describe all possible breaches with reference to the applicable section numbers within the standards of practice guidelines.
- What are some possible consequences for his actions? Did he have other options? If so, what were they?
- Do you think he would be blamed if he knew she had pills and immediately after the session she over-dosed? If so, please explain.

My response:

74

Ina works on the adult outpatient mental health team at a local hospital. She has been having regular sessions for the past five months with a 21-year-old woman regarding an eating/body image disorder. The client's mother was the source of referral, and she called today to ask Ina about her daughter's progress. Ina has never asked her client to sign consent forms for disclosure, but she knows that the client is very close to her mother and that she probably would not mind if Ina updated her mother. Ina decides to share information with the mother, and then simply have the client sign the release forms at her next appointment and back date them for the file.

- Was Ina's decision ethical?
- If it *was*, please explain why.
- If it *was not*, what is your reasoning? If she breached the code of ethics that you are required to follow, describe all possible breaches with reference to the applicable section numbers within the standards of practice guidelines.
- How might her client feel and act if she did not want her mother updated? What recourse does she have?
- What could Ina have done or said instead?

My response:

75

Karindeep works at a nonprofit family counseling agency in an inner-city neighborhood that has a four-month waitlist for services. Once one case is closed and the clinician is ready to open a new one, the next client folder, containing the client profile and phone intake information, is pulled by the social worker so the initial call to invite the client in can be made. The files are located in a cabinet, with the next file to be picked up always at the end of the row. When Karindeep opens the drawer and pulls the next file on the waitlist, she sees that the name on the file sounds Jewish. She puts it back and takes the next file beside it instead, which does not have a traditional Jewish name on it.

- Was it unethical for Karindeep to not take the first file?
- If it was *ethical*, explain your reasoning.
- If it was *unethical*, please explain your position. If she breached the code of ethics that you are required to follow, describe all possible breaches with reference to the applicable section numbers within the standards of practice guidelines.
- What if Karindeep did take the first file and was disrespectful to the client? Would this be a case of countertransference? Why or why not?

My response:

76

Erin works at a shelter for battered women and has developed a strong emotional investment in one particular woman for whom she feels quite sad because of the cruelty that she has had to live through. Over several weeks, a powerful drive grew in Erin to actually lay eyes on the man who dehumanized and terrorized her client to such a degree. Just thinking about him made her blood boil. It brought back many dark memories of her own past of witnessing violence in her childhood home and, later, of being a victim of it at the hands of her then-husband. Erin jotted down her client's home address at the end of her shift at the shelter and decided to drive by the house to hopefully get a glimpse of her client's common-law husband. She saw a man working under the hood of a car parked in the driveway who met the general description given to her by the client. Erin parked across the road and stared at him while a flashback of her past overwhelmed her senses, thoughts, and feelings. When she re-grounded, Erin got out of her car and with angry determination, she threw a rock at him, and then stormed over to confront the man, throwing an extreme verbal and physical barrage at him during the confrontation.

- Did Erin engage in unethical behavior?
- If her behavior was *ethical*, please explain why.
- If it was *unethical*, share your position. If Erin breached the code of ethics that you are required to follow, describe all possible breaches with reference to the applicable section numbers within the standards of practice guidelines.
- What do you think the impact of her actions could be for her client?

My response:

77

Patricia works in palliative care at a hospital and assisted a family in the dying days of an 88-year-old woman. When she finally died, two of her grandchildren, both in their early 20s, entered the room and started bickering over her personal effects. One of them removed a pearl necklace from around the neck of the deceased, while another took two rings off her fingers, both gold with inlaid jewels. Patricia told them to stop what they were doing and blocked the door. She then called for security, creating quite a scene on this generally quiet ward.

- Did Patricia make an ethically sound decision?
- If you believe that it was *ethical*, what convinced you?
- If she acted *unethically*, please explain your position. If she breached the code of ethics that you are required to follow, describe all possible breaches with reference to the applicable section numbers within the standards of practice guidelines.
- Was her client the deceased woman, the family, or both? Please share your thoughts.
- What, if any, responsibility do you still hold after your client dies?
- What would you have done? Do you think there were grounds for a "citizen's arrest"?

My response:

78

Krisztian was diagnosed with Bipolar Affective Disorder last year after a manic episode that involved paranoid, delusional thinking. He was in the hospital for 10 days but recovered very well. He has been stable on medication since the incident. Because he has been doing so well, he decided to stop taking his medication. Krisztian never told his employer or his colleagues why he was really away from work, claiming instead that he had had his appendix removed. They remained unaware of his diagnosis and of the medication he had been taking. Krisztian works at a hospital as its Chief Privacy Officer and increasingly, he has been acting very secretive, checking his office for cameras and listening devices every time he returns to it, and demanding unusual, even bizarre policy changes at the hospital.

- Is it ethical for Krisztian to keep his mental health issues private?
- If his behavior *is* ethical, please explain why.
- If it *is not* ethical, share your position. If Krisztian is breaching the code of ethics that you are required to follow, describe all possible breaches with reference to the applicable section numbers within the standards of practice guidelines.
- When, if ever, is it appropriate to share your medical or mental health history with your employer, and when, if ever, is it required?
- If Krisztian refuses to take sick leave to deal with his mental health issues, which he does not acknowledge, what other options do his employers have?

My response:

79

John is a child protection manager in a large and busy metropolitan area. In part, his job is to oversee a district that is covered by 25 protection workers in two teams, each with his or her own supervisor. Their caseloads are "bursting at the seams," and he has done all he can to provide additional support. He has rearranged some of the administrative procedures to ease the pressure and workload on his staff as much as possible. They have a triage system in which "urgent" referrals are seen within 12 hours, "high risk" within 48 hours, "serious" within a week, and "moderate" and "low risk" in up to six months. As a result of legislative changes, the definition of child abuse in his state has expanded to include *all* forms of corporal punishment, all forms of emotional abuse, and all cases in which children are in the presence of illegal drugs. No extra money has been allocated to John's department, despite the huge increase expected in the volume of referrals. John decides that "moderate" and "low risk" referrals will be investigated by phone only from this point forward, and one staff person will be assigned to clear the backlog with a two-week deadline in preparation for the influx of new referrals.

- Was John's solution ethical?
- If it *was*, please explain why.
- If it *was not*, share your thoughts. If John breached the code of ethics that you are required to follow, describe all possible breaches with reference to the applicable section numbers within the standards of practice guidelines.
- What is the possible impact of this administrative decision?
- How might his employees feel? How ethical will their practice be under these new rules?

My response:

80

Charmaine is an assistant professor of social work at a small Midwestern university. One of her female students in her policy class has requested extra attention from her almost from the start of the term, frequently waiting to see her after class to ask for clarification on concepts learned that day, and often seeing her during office time seeking help on assignments or to chat about her career prospects. They recently met over lunch in the school's cafeteria, at which time the student took a chance and opened up about her interests and personal beliefs on a number of subjects. Charmaine started to feel quite comfortable with this bright student, who seemed to share her interests and values. It was not long after this lunch that they started to date one another, but not openly.

- Would this behavior be considered ethical?
- If it *is* ethical, please explain your reasoning.
- If it *is not*, describe your position. If Charmaine breached the code of ethics that you are required to follow, describe all possible breaches with reference to the applicable section numbers within the standards of practice guidelines.
- If they break up, who has the most to lose and why?
- Which of them has the most power in this relationship? Please explain.
- Who is the one who holds the most responsibility for setting and maintaining professional boundaries? Why?

My response:

May not be reproduced without permission of the publisher. Please use additional sheets if necessary.

81

Bruce works at an outpatient clinic and receives a call from a detective sergeant from the local police department. He is asked if Jane Doe is a client who actively attends the clinic. Ms. Doe is not on his caseload, but he remembers from team meeting that she is on a co-worker's caseload, and the co-worker is currently on vacation. Bruce is careful not to give too much information, but he does confirm that Ms. Doe is a current client. The detective then asks Bruce to look up when she is scheduled for her next appointment, because the police need to arrest her for outstanding warrants. As a dutiful member of society, Bruce looks on the centralized booking system and sees that she is due to come in this coming Monday at 3 p.m., which he passes on to the detective. Bruce does not document this event in the client's chart, as he does not consider it clinical in nature.

- Was this behavior ethical?
- If it *was*, please explain your reasoning.
- If it *was not*, describe your position. If he breached the code of ethics that you are required to follow, describe all possible breaches with reference to the applicable section numbers within the standards of practice guidelines.
- What does the privacy legislation that you are required to follow say about what can and cannot be disclosed to the police with or without a search warrant?
- When is informed consent for disclosure necessary in cases like this one?

My response:

82

Michelle works at a nonprofit community-based agency that offers a program for new immigrant women to develop social supports, learn the language, and better understand the culture of the host community and country. Many of the women with school-aged children bring their children with them when the schools have the day off. On these days, they all help to prepare a community meal of traditional North American dishes, which they eat together. A Filipino mother and her two sons, ages five and eight, were sitting across from Michelle when she witnessed the two boys mushing their food into their spoons with their forks before gobbling it down. Michelle felt disgusted and offended by what appeared to be a case of poor table manners rather than a traditional way of eating in the Philippines. She told the mother that she needed to teach her children to be more civilized, and then turned to the children and said in a sharp tone, "Stop eating like animals!"

- Did Michelle act in an ethical manner?
- If it was *ethical*, explain your reasoning.
- If she was acting *unethically*, please explain your position. If she breached the code of ethics that you are required to follow, describe all possible breaches with reference to the applicable section numbers within the standards of practice guidelines.
- How might the mother feel? How might her children feel?

My response:

83

Omar runs a private practice with a central office location. He is situated on the second floor within an older three-story walk-up style office building with no elevating device. A prospective client called him last week and arranged an initial consultation for today. Five minutes after the scheduled time for the new client to arrive, Omar received a phone call from the client stating that he was out front but could not get up the steps to the front door. Omar met the client outside and found that the man was in a motorized wheelchair. With no prospect of getting the man up to his office, Omar told him that he could not help him.

- Was Omar's decision ethical?
- If it *was*, please explain why.
- If it *was not*, share your thoughts. If Omar breached the code of ethics that you are required to follow, describe all possible breaches with reference to the applicable section numbers within the standards of practice guidelines.
- What is Omar's responsibility in terms of having a wheelchair accessible office?
- Should he announce to every prospective client that his office is not wheelchair accessible? Should he ask every prospective client if he or she is disabled? What are the implications?
- Can you think of other solutions to this problem that also retain the dignity of the client?

My response:

84

Dara is the sole proprietor of a private practice that specializes in life coaching for individuals and couples. One of her regular clients was recently laid off from the auto service center where she worked and, therefore, she can no longer afford to pay Dara her regular fee. The client is a mechanic by trade, and she and Dara strike a deal that the client will do some repair work on Dara's car in exchange for three individual sessions.

- Would Dara's deal be considered ethical?
- If it *is* ethical, please explain your reasoning.
- If it *is not*, describe your position. If she breached the code of ethics that you are required to follow, describe all possible breaches with reference to the applicable section numbers within the standards of practice guidelines.
- What services or objects can be ethically bartered for in exchange for social work services?

My response:

85

Doug is a consultant who works with nonprofit agencies to help them increase efficiency and decrease costs in the delivery of services to their consumers. While working on a new contract with an agency that provides emergency shelter to homeless and transitioning consumers, he learned from the executive director that last month, they had to fire a licensed social worker because of evidence of inappropriate sexual relations between the worker and a homeless client. Doug asked the executive director if the worker's regulatory body had been informed or if the police had investigated. The reply was "no," and Doug sensed a lot of resistance to the idea, possibly because of the bad press the agency would receive as a result. Doug had the name of the worker and considered calling the regulatory body himself to inform them of the allegations, but he decided not to, because it would be obvious to the executive director that he was the one who made the call. He knew that if he did call, he would surely lose the contract with that agency.

- Was Doug's decision not to make the call an ethical one?
- If it *was*, please explain why.
- If it *was not*, share your thoughts. If Doug breached the code of ethics that you are required to follow, describe all possible breaches with reference to the applicable section numbers within the standards of practice guidelines.
- What are the possible consequences of reporting or not reporting?
- What would you have done if you were Doug?

My response:

86

Lisa works on a multidisciplinary intervention team that works with new mothers and their premature babies. During a home visit that she provided by herself, she was very critical of the mother's parenting skills, calling her incompetent and taking over from the mother when the baby's diaper needed to be changed, when he was hungry, and during burping. Lisa often showed visible frustration watching the mother before screeching, "Oh, just let me do it!" Lisa had only negative things to say about the cleanliness of the house, as well, calling the mother "lazy." She told the mother that if the apartment was not clean to her satisfaction by the next visit, she would be calling child protective services.

- Did Lisa engage in unethical behavior?
- If her behavior was *ethical,* please explain why.
- If it was *unethical,* share your position. If Lisa breached the code of ethics that you are required to follow, describe all possible breaches with reference to the applicable section numbers within the standards of practice guidelines.
- Do you think Lisa's behavior would have been different if the rest of her multidisciplinary team had been present and watching her?
- What do you think the effect of her behavior might be on this young mother?
- Given the mother's struggles, what underlying mental health problem should Lisa be assessing for rather than just providing criticism?

My response:

May not be reproduced without permission of the publisher. Please use additional sheets if necessary.

87

Hans runs a small private practice with three associates. He discovered that one of his clients wrote him two NSF (nonsufficient funds) checks in a row for her last two sessions, and the bank has charged him $40 in service fees for handling the bad checks. When he called his client, she said she was unaware of the problem but swore to Hans that at the next session she would give him the outstanding $240 in cash, plus the $40 in service fees for the two bad checks, per their contract. The session time came and went without a word from her. She now owed a total of $400, because she did not give notice that she was cancelling the appointment. Hans tried calling her several times, but the only number he had for her kept sending him to voicemail, which was full. He sent two letters to her address by registered mail asking to be paid, with a warning that she would be taken to small claims court or a collection agency would be retained. There was no response, so Hans called a collection agency and provided them with all of her contact information, a copy of their contract, and information on the nature of his service. On his behalf, the agency harassed the client until she agreed to settle her account with Hans.

* Would this behavior be considered ethical?
* If it *was* ethical, please share your reasoning.
* If it *was not*, explain your position. If Hans breached the code of ethics that you are required to follow, describe all possible breaches with reference to the applicable section numbers within the standards of practice guidelines.
* Would it have been better for Hans to take her to small claims court? Why or why not? If yes, what if he arranged for the case to be heard on national TV in front of Judge Judy? What potential ethical problems would you foresee?
* If you thought that Hans behaved unethically, how would you suggest he recoup his earned, but missing, $400?

My response:

88

Jennifer is a supervisor of foster homes. Once a month, she must do a home visit to ensure the homes remain in good order and to ensure that the foster parents are supported, often solving problems on the fly. She has a good working relationship with the Wojohowitz family, who are dairy farmers. Sometimes she greets the foster children if they are around, but it is not part of her role to talk to them, as they each have their own worker and are seen regularly. Mr. and Mrs. Wojohowitz are most concerned that Cheri, their 5-year-old foster daughter, has not been bathing, and as a result, she smells of cow dung. This is complicated by the fact that Cheri's biological mother calls her every night and undermines Mr. and Mrs. Wojohowitz by telling her not to bathe or brush her teeth because it is against their religion. The foster parents want permission to cut off contact between Cheri and her mother. Cheri wants more contact with her mother and wants to move back in with her. The biological mother does not want her daughter home yet because she considers her a burden, but would like to visit Cheri more often. Cheri is in care on a voluntary contract with child protective services, not by court order. Jennifer feels obliged to support the foster parents and agrees to the plan to stop the daily phone contact between mother and daughter. The mother claims that she and Cheri are being discriminated against based on their religious beliefs.

- Did Jennifer make an ethically sound decision?
- If *yes*, please share your thoughts.
- If *no*, explain your position. If she breached the code of ethics that you are required to follow, describe all possible breaches with reference to the applicable section numbers within the standards of practice guidelines.
- Who is Jennifer's primary client? The child? The biological mother? The foster parents? Someone else? To what degree should each of their opinions inform her decision?
- How might consulting with a supervisor help in this case?

My response:

89

Jasmine is a manager at a custodial treatment center for youth who have been convicted of crimes such as assault, burglary, arson, and car theft. She runs three homes on two different sites, managing all day-to-day affairs, plus the supervision of front-line caregivers and clinical staff. Other than shift leads, there are no supervisors below her to share her workload. Her staff members are already regularly working overtime as it is, so they cannot be asked to take on some of her more mundane responsibilities. She has complained to the executive director that she is overworked and more staff members need to be hired, but there is no money in the budget for anyone new. Jasmine is proud of her employees, who are well qualified, very competent, and do a great job working with the youth. Although she knows that they require regular clinical supervision, there is always something else that comes up, and appointments are usually cancelled. She feels crushed by the competing pressures of her job, and supervision keeps falling off the agenda. Some of the senior staff members have not had supervision in a year, Jasmine finally admitted to the executive director with shame.

- Was Jasmine's decision to let supervision slide ethical?
- If it *was*, please explain your reasoning.
- If it *was not*, explain your position. If she breached the code of ethics that you are required to follow, describe all possible breaches with reference to the applicable section numbers within the standards of practice guidelines.
- What do you think the effect of little or no clinical supervision has on the professional development of the workers, their morale, and their ability to cope with the stresses of the job? Would Jasmine lose the respect of her employees if she did not provide supervision regularly?
- Do you believe she undervalued the importance of supervision and should have reprioritized her workload? Should she have informed the ED of her struggles sooner? Please explain.

My response:

90

David works at a mental health clinic on a Native American reservation. He started a private practice and hoped to eventually build up his clientele to the point that he could quit his job at the clinic and finally work for himself. David gave every client he saw at the clinic, whether it was his own or one of his colleagues', his business card and a warm handshake while he told them about the benefits of switching over to his private services. During his lunch hour, while the receptionist was away, he pulled out the waitlist from behind her desk and photocopied the list, so he could call those people to invite them to his practice, as well.

- Would David's actions be considered ethical?
- If they are *ethical*, please explain why.
- If they are *unethical*, describe your reasoning. If David breached the code of ethics that you are required to follow, describe all possible breaches with reference to the applicable section numbers within the standards of practice guidelines.
- What impact, if any, might his actions have on the clients at the clinic?
- How might David's actions negatively affect the clinic for which he worked?

My response:

91

Pauline is a social work officer in the U.S. Army and is currently stationed in Iraq. She finds her job very stressful and morally confusing. Pauline is a pacifist and joined the Army to help pay off her hefty student loans, but now she feels complicit in a war she considers to be illegal. For six months, she hid her feelings and compartmentalized her traumatic experiences (often gained vicariously through her work with the soldier clients). One morning, after a fitful sleep with multiple nightmares, Pauline decided that she could no longer do her job. She could not stand the thought of her skills as a social worker being used by the war machine to help soldiers return to the fight to needlessly kill more people or be killed themselves. In her civilian clothing, she went to her headquarters and demanded to be repatriated immediately.

- Did Pauline handle this issue in an ethical manner?
- If she *did,* please explain why.
- If *not,* share your thoughts. If Pauline breached the code of ethics that you are required to follow, describe all possible breaches with reference to the applicable section numbers within the standards of practice guidelines.
- How might her behavior affect her clients?

My response:

92

Krista is the acting manager at a shelter for abused women. On Tuesday night, someone called the emergency line requesting a bed right away. Krista was paged at home and took over the call at the request of the crisis worker, because it was "an unusual one." She called the person back, who identified herself as "Frank," stating that she wanted out of an abusive relationship with her husband and needed a safe place to stay until she could make other arrangements. She also expressed a need for emotional support and information on other community services and steps she could take to remain safe. Krista was skeptical of the person's claims and decided that it was a hoax. She asked Frank for her true gender, and challenged that she had a deep voice like a man and had a typical man's name. She pointed out that the primary mandate of the shelter is to protect women and their children from abusive men. Frank informed her that she was a transsexual and again told her that she needed protection. Krista sternly told Frank that if she wanted help, she needed to go somewhere else because the shelter had no room for "sickos" like her. Two days later, Krista heard on the radio that a man had been arrested in the stabbing death of his partner, a 42-year-old transsexual named Frank.

* Did Krista manage this situation ethically?
* If *yes*, please share your thoughts.
* If *no*, explain your position. If she breached the code of ethics that you are required to follow, describe all possible breaches with reference to the applicable section numbers within the standards of practice guidelines.
* How might you have handled this differently, even if you absolutely could not allow Frank into the shelter?
* If Frank was allowed to stay at the shelter, what might the impact be on the other residents? Could this set a precedent whereby the shelter might start to get referrals from heterosexual men? What could the implications be if this trend caught on?

My response:

93

Phineas is a social worker who provides general counseling to individuals and couples. One of his clients wanted his lawyer to obtain a copy of the social work assessment on him that Phineas had recently completed writing. The client signed a release form to allow this disclosure and then gave Phineas a business card with a lawyer's name and fax number on it. Phineas did not look at the card, other than to take down the fax number. It was only after Phineas faxed the report that the client realized that he had given Phineas the card for his estranged wife's lawyer, with whom he was in litigation, instead of his own lawyer's card. Based on the information disclosed in the report, his estranged wife's lawyer boosted the amount claimed for alimony and child support by 100%. The client is now furious with Phineas.

- Would Phineas' behavior be considered ethical?
- If it *is*, please explain your reasoning.
- If it *is not*, explain your position. If he breached the code of ethics that you are required to follow, describe all possible breaches with reference to the applicable section numbers within the standards of practice guidelines.
- Who do you think holds the greatest blame?
- Do you think the client has a case should he decide to sue Phineas?

My response:

94

Keith works at an urban core social agency and he is one of two social workers who provide a trustee service for consumers who cannot manage their money well and volunteer to allow the agency to hold and dole the cash out to them at regular intervals. Keith does not make much money, and he is often $100 short before payday comes. For the past year, he has been secretly borrowing from the accounts of the consumers, but is very careful to return every last penny once he gets paid.

- Would this behavior be considered ethical?
- If it *is* ethical, please explain your reasoning.
- If it *is not*, describe your position. If Keith breached the code of ethics that you are required to follow, describe all possible breaches with reference to the applicable section numbers within the standards of practice guidelines.
- If there is no negative impact on the clients, why would some say it is unethical?

My response:

May not be reproduced without permission of the publisher. Please use additional sheets if necessary.

95

Lori is a Caucasian social worker employed by adult protective services and provides welfare checks on senior citizens when family, friends, or neighbors call with concerns about a senior's care, safety, or accommodation. Lori is dispatched to a run-down neighborhood with a high rate of drug dealing, prostitution, robbery, and murder, to the house of an isolated 72-year-old man who has not been seen by neighbors in two weeks. When she knocks on his door, a very large African American man in his twenties answers the door and immediately tells her to get lost (but in more colorful terms) before she can get a word in edge-wise. Lori walks back to her car and documents that the man she went to see was home and the neighbors' concerns were unfounded. She writes that no follow-up is recommended.

- Did Lori act in an ethical manner?
- If she *did*, please explain your reasoning.
- If she *did not*, why not? If she breached the code of ethics that you are required to follow, describe all possible breaches with reference to the applicable section numbers within the standards of practice guidelines.
- If Lori truly was afraid for her safety, what alternatives did she have?
- Take the opposite view and argue for the opinion you did not initially take.
- What would you have done?

My response:

96

Dimitri is a medical social worker at a small general hospital in a rural town. He is clinically supervised by a medical doctor and administratively supervised by a nurse manager. He finds that he must keep advocating not only for his clients, but for the role of social work in the field of medicine, which is sometimes ignored or brushed off by other, more prominent and politically powerful disciplines. When a nurse on his unit arranges a family meeting for one of his patients without involving him, Dimitri is livid and loudly confronts the woman at the nursing station in full view and hearing of several patients and a couple of other staff.

- Did Dimitri engage in unethical behavior?
- If his behavior was *ethical*, please explain why.
- If it was *unethical*, share your position. If Dimitri breached the code of ethics that you are required to follow, describe all possible breaches with reference to the applicable section numbers within the standards of practice guidelines.
- What impact do you think this outburst might have had on the patients and staff?
- How could he have handled this situation differently?

My response:

May not be reproduced without permission of the publisher. Please use additional sheets if necessary.

97

Matt is an associate at a private practice. He has always had an interest in hypnotism and was intrigued with the notion that it could be used therapeutically with clients. He attended a one-day workshop presented by a dynamic clinician, whose name he could no longer remember. Pretty confident that he had the basic skills, he introduced to his clients the option of using hypnotherapy to deal with a number of issues, from smoking and weight loss to depression and anxiety. Matt receives external supervision, but the supervisor is not a qualified hypnotherapist.

- Would Matt's actions be considered ethical?
- If they *are* ethical, please explain why.
- If they *are not*, describe your reasoning. If Matt breached the code of ethics that you are required to follow, describe all possible breaches with reference to the applicable section numbers within the standards of practice guidelines.
- Would your opinion change if he had a hypnotist as a mentor, but she was not a psychotherapist?
- What impact, if any, might his actions have on the clients of the practice?

My response:

98

Armando is a tenured associate professor of social work at a prestigious university. Since joining the faculty 30 years ago, he has always been eccentric and arrogant. Armando's research, which he has regularly talked about in his classes, has shifted away from ideals of a "social safety net" and toward a more conservative view of "survival of the fittest" within society. His writing and teaching increasingly express intolerant messages that the poor, disabled, and disenfranchised should be left to their own devices while resources should instead be directed toward those with more potential and motivation to benefit society. Enrollment in his classes has declined, and his peers rebuke him. He has no intention of resigning any time soon.

- Is Armando engaging in unethical behavior?
- If his behavior is *ethical,* please explain why.
- If it is *unethical,* share your position. If Armando breached the code of ethics that you are required to follow, describe all possible breaches with reference to the applicable section numbers within the standards of practice guidelines.
- What are Armando's rights and what are his responsibilities in his position?
- Is there a line where intellectual freedom conflicts with ethics? Where do you think it lies?

My response:

99

Andrew has a regular client with whom he meets every week to work on issues of passive suicidal ideation, cutting, and self-mutilation. The client also e-mails him at work, usually once or twice a week, sending him blog entrics and other postings that complain about her miserable, hopeless life. Andrew does not have the knowledge or skills to encrypt his e-mails, and he knows that confidentiality cannot be maintained, but he presumes that his client is waiving this protection by e-mailing him first. He replies back to her e-mails with suggestions and always a reminder to use her crisis plan if she needs it. Although he is careful not to mention the client's name when he replies, a lot of her identifying information is sent back to her over the Internet, including the original e-mail to which he responded.

- Would this behavior be considered ethical?
- If it *would* be, please explain your reasoning.
- If it *is not,* describe your position. If he breached the code of ethics that you are required to follow, describe all possible breaches with reference to the applicable section numbers within the standards of practice guidelines.
- What would you do if you were Andrew?

My response:

100

Barika is an unemployed social worker who took several years off to raise her children. She was still licensed and wanted to re-enter the field, so she decided to do some volunteer work to build some more recent experience for her résumé. She found a position at a local food bank. It was Barika's job to check the identification of the people coming in for food hampers and compare it to the list to ensure that it had been at least four weeks since they had last received one. Those who came in looked so downtrodden and ashamed at having to ask for assistance, that Barika could not will herself to further bother them with having to show ID. Many of them said they did not have any ID anyway. By mid-morning, Barika was giving out hampers to everyone who came in, and she occasionally added a few extra things to the hamper if the people looked particularly malnourished.

- Did Barika act in an ethical manner?
- If she *did,* please explain your reasoning.
- If she *did not,* why not? If she breached the code of ethics that you are required to follow, describe all possible breaches with reference to the applicable section numbers within the standards of practice guidelines.
- What is the possible impact of her behavior?
- Would you hire her? Why or why not?

My response:

May not be reproduced without permission of the publisher. Please use additional sheets if necessary.

101

Clariss works with teenagers at an alternative school for high school students expelled from their regular schools. Most of the youths seem to appreciate her help, because she is easy-going and not an authority figure in their eyes. One of the 10th grade students, Whitney, is always pleasant with Clariss and often wants her undivided attention. On Friday night, when Clariss was at home checking her social networks online, she received a friend request from Whitney. Clariss smiled with recognition of her name and clicked "Accept" to add her to her friends list.

- Was there anything unethical about Clariss' decision?
- If she remained *ethical,* please explain your reasoning.
- If she *did not,* describe how her behavior was unethical. If Clariss breached the code of ethics that you are required to follow, describe all possible breaches with reference to the applicable section numbers within the standards of practice guidelines.
- What message do you think Clariss' behavior sent to Whitney?

My response:

Create Your Own Scenarios

The next pages are provided for you to write and discuss your own scenarios. These may come from your own social work practice, field placement, students, colleagues, or from your imagination.

Scenario:

Discussion:

May not be reproduced without permission of the publisher. Please use additional sheets if necessary.

Scenario:

Discussion:

Scenario:

Discussion:

May not be reproduced without permission of the publisher. Please use additional sheets if necessary.

Scenario:

Discussion:

Scenario:

Discussion:

Scenario:

Discussion:

Select Listing of National and International Codes of Ethics for Social Workers

The following list consists of Web links to codes of ethics for professional social workers. Please note that state licensing boards and other credentialing agencies often have their own codes of ethics or codes of conduct, to which those who hold the credential are bound. Schools of social work and employers also may have their own codes. Please check with your licensing or credentialing board, school of social work, professional association, or employer if you are unsure about which code you are required to follow.

Aotearoa New Zealand Association of Social Workers
http://anzasw.org.nz/sw-in-nz/code-of-ethics/

Association of Social Workers India
http://socialworker.net.in/page.php?5

Australian Association of Social Workers
http://www.aasw.asn.au/publications/ethics-and-standards

British Association of Social Workers
http://www.basw.co.uk/about/code-of-ethics/

Canadian Association of Social Workers
http://www.casw-acts.ca/canada/codepage_e.html

International Federation of Social Workers
http://www.ifsw.org/f38000032.html

Irish Association of Social Workers
http://www.iasw.ie/index.php/press-releases/13-joomla/15-iasw-code-of-ethics

National Association of Social Workers (U.S.A.)
http://www.naswdc.org/pubs/code/code.asp

South African Occupational Social Workers' Association
http://www.saoswa.org.za/ethics.htm

Select List of Journals on Ethics

The following are examples of journals that publish articles about social work ethics and related topics.

Asian Journal of Professional Ethics & Management
http://www.ethicsasiajournal.com/

Journal of Clinical Ethics
http://www.clinicalethics.com/

Journal of Social Work Values and Ethics
http://www.socialworker.com/jswve

Index

NOTE: *The scenarios identified below are connected to the headings in some cases based loosely on the* potential *that they might fall into that category, sometimes just because of the questions raised by the author. Numbers represent the scenario number, not the page number.*

Duty to the Client/Public - 14, 17, 18, 24, 26, 27, 28, 29, 32, 33, 37, 38, 40, 41,48, 49, 50, 52, 53, 55, 56, 58, 59, 61, 62, 63, 64, 73, 76, 77, 81, 83, 85, 86, 88, 89, 90, 91, 92, 93, 95, 96, 97

Financial Issues - 20, 28, 35, 67, 84, 87, 93, 94

Gender/Sexual Orientation Issues - 14, 21, 46, 51, 92

Gifts & Favors - 4, 7, 9, 16, 19, 35, 51, 57, 64, 67, 84

Integrity - 4, 5, 8, 11, 12, 15, 16, 17, 18, 19, 22, 23, 24, 25, 30, 31, 33, 34, 35, 37, 38, 41, 43, 44, 47, 52, 54, 56, 57, 59, 62, 66, 67, 71, 72, 74, 80, 90, 91, 94, 95, 96

Physical Assault - 10, 11, 54, 73, 76

Religion/Politics - 27, 40, 42, 88

Scope of Practice/Competence - 30, 37, 43, 44, 69, 76, 78, 86, 91, 97

Self-Determination - 10, 14, 17, 32, 40, 61, 73, 82

Self-Harm/Suicide - 41, 73, 99

Sexual Misconduct - 3, 33, 36, 46, 54, 73, 80

Supervision - 3, 25, 35, 37, 53, 55, 69, 72, 78, 88, 89, 97

About the Author

 Thomas Horn is a *Registered Social Worker* (RSW) with both the *Ontario College of Social Workers and Social Service Workers* (OCSWSSW) in Ontario, Canada, and the *General Social Care Council* (GSCC) in England. Tom is also a Graduate Member of the British Psychological Society. He has been working in the social services field for more than 20 years in a variety of settings, including residential developmental care, residential and outpatient child and adolescent mental health, residential drug/alcohol treatment, and inpatient psychiatry. Currently, Tom works with an inpatient forensic mental health team at a large psychiatric hospital in Ontario. He routinely provides field supervision to social work students at the undergraduate and graduate levels. He is a single father of two boys with special needs.

ALSO PUBLISHED BY
WHITE HAT COMMUNICATIONS:

BOOKS

Days in the Lives of Social Workers
edited by Linda May Grobman

More Days in the Lives of Social Workers
edited by Linda May Grobman

Days in the Lives of Gerontological Social Workers
edited by Linda May Grobman and Dara Bergel Bourassa

The Field Placement Survival Guide
edited by Linda May Grobman

The Social Work Graduate School Applicant's Handbook
by Jesús Reyes

An Introduction to the Nonprofit Sector:
A Practical Approach for the Twenty-First Century
by Gary M. Grobman

The Nonprofit Handbook
by Gary M. Grobman

The Nonprofit Management Casebook
by Gary M. Grobman

MAGAZINE
The New Social Worker Magazine

VISIT OUR WEB SITES
www.socialworker.com
www.socialworkjobbank.com
www.whitehatcommunications.com

NETWORK WITH US
www.facebook.com/newsocialworker
www.facebook.com/whitehatcommunications
www.twitter.com/newsocialworker

ORDER FORM

I would like to order the following:

Qty.	Item	Price
_____	Days in the Lives of Social Workers @ $19.95	_____
_____	More Days in the Lives of Social Workers @ $16.95	_____
_____	Field Placement Survival Guide @ $22.95	_____
_____	Social Work Grad. School App. Hdbk. @ $19.95	_____
_____	Days in the Lives/Geron. Social Workers @ $19.95	_____
_____	Is It Ethical? 101 Scenarios @ $14.95	_____

Please send my order to:

Name _____

Organization _____

Address _____

City_____ State_____ Zip _____

Telephone_____

Please send me more information about ❏social work and ❏nonprofit management publications available from White Hat Communications.

Sales tax: Please add 6% sales tax for books shipped to Pennsylvania addresses.

Shipping/handling:
❏Books sent to U.S. addresses: $8.50 first book/$1.50 each add'l book.
❏Books sent to Canada: $12.00 per book.
❏Books sent to addresses outside the U.S. and Canada: Please contact us for rates.

Payment:
Check or money order enclosed for $_____
U.S. funds only.

Please charge my: ❏MC ❏Visa ❏AMEX ❏Discover

Card #: _____

Expiration Date _____ 3- or 4-digit CVV _____

Name on card: _____

Billing address (if different from above): _____

_____

Signature: _____

Mail this form with payment to:
WHITE HAT COMMUNICATIONS, P.O. Box 5390, Dept. E
Harrisburg, PA 17110-0390
Questions? Call 717-238-3787.
Credit card orders: call 717-238-3787 or fax 717-238-2090
or order online at http://shop.whitehatcommunications.com